Praise for
GRACE IN THE GRAY

"Because grace is beautiful, I think God designed us for beautiful relationships. Sometimes relationships are hard. That is what my friend Mike Donehey has accomplished in his new book, *Grace in the Gray*—a way to love and discuss hard things the way Jesus would."
—BOB GOFF, *New York Times* bestselling author of
Love Does, Dream Big, and *Undistracted*

"I've had the privilege of knowing Mike Donehey for many years now and have always felt that he is one of the most thoughtful lyricists and communicators I know. Mike is a thinker, but so much more than that, he is a lover of people. Written with just the right amount of humor, reflection, and heart, *Grace in the Gray* shows us how to focus on the people we may disagree with more than focusing on the issue at hand."
—MAC POWELL, Grammy Award–winning
singer and songwriter

"In a world that is seemingly more divided and polarized than ever, Mike stands out as a peacemaker. He has a unique gift of reaching across the divides and reminding people with his own vulnerability that we are all created and loved by the same God."
—GARETH AND ALI GILKESON, Rend Collective

"Who is waiting for you when the road rises up and smacks you in the face, when life sneaks up and hits you from behind and knocks you to your knees? Mike Donehey realized it was from these positions that he was in the best place to reach out for God's hand and rise up. From accidents and intentions, decadence to ascension, his life and God's will found a place called home."

—KEN MANSFIELD, author, producer, and former
US manager of the Beatles' Apple Records

"At times in our friendship, God has used Mike to tell me exactly what I need to hear at just the right moment. I believe many will feel that Mike has done the same for them after reading *Finding God's Life for My Will*. Reading Mike's words is like getting a new eyeglass prescription. You'll see Jesus and life with new clarity, and the result will be joy, freedom, and peace. This is a great read for anyone looking to take a next step with Jesus while laughing along the way."

—TIMOTHY ATEEK, teaching pastor at
Watermark Community Church

"Challenging, captivating, and convicting. In *Finding God's Life for My Will*, Mike not only offers a refreshing perspective, but he also gives us the wisdom we need to really live the life we were always made for!"

—JORDAN LEE DOOLEY, author of *Own Your Everyday*
and host of the *SHE* podcast

GRACE
IN THE
GRAY

GRACE
IN THE
GRAY

A MORE LOVING WAY
TO DISAGREE

MIKE DONEHEY

WATERBROOK

Published in the United States by WaterBrook, an imprint of Random House, a division of Penguin Random House LLC.

WATERBROOK® and its deer colophon are registered trademarks of Penguin Random House LLC.

Library of Congress Cataloging-in-Publication Data
Names: Donehey, Mike, author.
Title: Grace in the gray: a more loving way to disagree / Mike Donehey.
Description: First edition. | Colorado Springs: WaterBrook, [2023]
Identifiers: LCCN 2022031364 (print) | LCCN 2022031365 (ebook) |
ISBN 9780593194188 (trade paperback; acid-free paper) | ISBN 9780593194195 (ebook)
Subjects: LCSH: Conflict management—Religious aspects—Christianity. |
Interpersonal relations—Religious aspects—Christianity.
Classification: LCC BV4597.53.C58 D66 2023 (print) | LCC BV4597.53.C58 (ebook) |
DDC 158.2—dc23/eng/20220907
LC record available at https://lccn.loc.gov/2022031364
LC ebook record available at https://lccn.loc.gov/2022031365

Printed in the United States of America on acid-free paper

waterbrookmultnomah.com

2 4 6 8 9 7 5 3 1

First Edition

Book design by Elizabeth A. D. Eno

Title page art by EvgeniiasArt/stock.adobe.com

SPECIAL SALES Most WaterBrook books are available at special quantity discounts when purchased in bulk by corporations, organizations, and special-interest groups. Custom imprinting or excerpting can also be done to fit special needs. For information, please email specialmarketscms@penguinrandomhouse.com.

For Kelly.

More than any other, God's grace through you has made me gracious. This book would never be without you.

CONTENTS

The Art of Elegant Disagreement

My wife is really good at disagreeing with me. I'm sure I'm not unique in this experience. But what might be unique is that I've learned to love it. Well, I'm learning to love it. I'll be posting a video online or texting some advice to a friend, and she'll joyfully stride in, peek over my shoulder, and say, "Are you sure you want to say it like that?"

I used to cringe at those words, but even though it's taken me years, I've come to welcome her critique. It helps that she's tactful, but trust me when I say that learning to love her dissent has been a journey in and of itself. I would even say that learning to love her opposing point of view has been instrumental in the writing of this book. Her considerations helped shift my initial idea. This book started out as something else entirely.

At first, I thought this was going to be a book outlining my personal positions on divisive topics. I was going to address every controversial matter the world has ever known. I'd do extensive research. I'd do a deep dive into a myriad of commentaries. I would eventually dazzle you with such scholastic brilliance that you'd realize my conclusions were so astute and insurmountable you wouldn't even dream of drawing any others. (I'm sorry if that's what you were hoping for. I really did try.)

I would begin with the topic of alcohol—a perfect choice because the opinions on drinking, at least within the church worlds I've been a part of, are varied and can be vitriolic. I even had a great chapter title: "Help! My Girlfriend Ordered a Beer!" Building off a true story, I would woo and wow you into complete agreement. *Brilliant, right?* Because of my expansive research and ingenious insights, I was certain a new humanity full of peace and understanding would undoubtedly emerge. I was going to solve the alcohol conundrum, and millions of relationships that had been broken because of the issue would be restored. *Hallelujah.* Once I wrapped up my bulletproof treatise on alcohol, I would move on to refugees and then politics and then vaccines, just for fun. Through this book, I was certain I would lead a unifying movement within the church and out in the world that would never again be rivaled. Or so I thought.

You know what happened?

My wife read it. She said, "I don't know if you've really covered the argument." I read it over. I cried inside; I didn't want her to see she was right. I had second thoughts. I began to wonder, *Maybe certain topics are divisive for good reasons. Maybe both sides of controversy have pretty good arguments. I know what stance I would take, but does my viewpoint necessarily negate the other side's? Will my conclusions lead to greater displays of grace and unity, or will they just become another bullet in the chamber for one side to blast the other?*

I ruminated.

I prayed.

I repented.

I decided against it.

I pivoted.

I rejoiced.

WHY GRACE IN THE GRAY?

My positions might have been sound, but my posture had a lot of growing up to do. I ended up calling this *Grace in the Gray* because I began to think that maybe God left some gray spaces on purpose. Maybe God wove some mystery into the world because He's more interested in cultivating great lovers than He is great debaters. And when I say great lovers, I don't mean the honeymoon-infatuation type. Falling in love is the easy part. It's all color and sparks. That's not the love I'm aiming for. Perhaps God wants us to learn to stay in love, even when it's hard, even when it's complicated. Even when it's long and arduous and not all black and white. Maybe staying in love truly is an art form all to itself. Yeah, I think that's it.

This book is about learning the artful elegance of loving one another in the gray spaces.

After all, gray is everywhere we look.

Try to resist it, but there's no escaping the truth.

The world is not always black and white.

Live just a little and you'll find it's true.

In fact, the gray isn't just in the way we see things.

The gray spaces are all around us.

They are built into the very fabric of the universe.

They are where the horizon lines disappear.

They are where the sky bleeds into the sea.

The gray is in the early morning fog rising off the rivers.

The gray spaces are in the skies above us.

God built them into the earth and sky and stars.

At dusk, when does the day end and the night begin?

At dawn, where is the sun when it's still behind the hills?

Solar pathways, lunar movements . . . we marvel when the sun is eclipsed and the light gives way to gray.

The gray spaces are in between us.

They are in our theologies and attempts to understand.

They are clouded in our limited perspectives.

We set our courses for unavoidable collisions of color and consequence.

The gray spaces are like bumper guards.

We have unique upbringings. We have unique views. We have biases.

We have limitations that we are sorely unaware of.

Sometimes I wonder if God put a little gray in the world to keep us all from killing one another.

As we go about our everyday lives, we will undoubtedly find ourselves standing in gray places.

We can choose to go toe to toe, or we can help carry one another through.

That's the aim of this book.

This book is not about agreeing to disagree. I've never much liked that phrase. It sounds as if two parties have decided to momentarily lay down their arms until a better opportunity to shoot each other arises. No. This isn't a treatise on tolerating the people who infuriate us. It's not about living with the ones who annoy us. It's not about how to reach a truce in cold, mutual disappointment where neither side is able to prevail. It's not a book on the art of stalemate—it's not chess. I have more in mind than the silent pushing away from a cluttered board because neither party could envision a way forward.

This is a book about a different strategy altogether: How can we more lovingly disagree? It's about leaning in and longing to understand. It's about admitting when we're wrong and not always assuming our views are the correct ones. It's about curiosity and kindness and asking better questions. I don't just want to try on another man's shoes; I want to live in them for a while. I want to explore what it might look like to forge ahead in friendship when it feels impossible to do anything but retreat.

In the book of Ephesians, Paul says that Christ "himself is our peace, who has made us both one and has broken down in his flesh the dividing wall of hostility" (2:14). There's a whole lot to that sentence, but among other things, it means we have peace in the midst of misunderstanding. It means the body of God was broken so that our communities could be put back together. It means that the walls of hostility were torn down between parties who otherwise would never have gotten along. It means we get to worry more about building bridges rather than looking for ones to burn down.

Though nuance is never easy, I believe it's worth fighting for. And when we fight for love in the gray spaces, we might find we've stopped fighting one another.

WHERE ARE WE FIGHTING ONE ANOTHER?

I'm thinking here about denominations worshipping exactness.

I'm thinking about politics serving policies and forgetting about people.

I'm thinking about people disowning family instead of being devoted to them.

If Christ came to destroy the hostility between us, then that must mean there is a unity far deeper and more beautiful than anything we have settled for thus far.

The purpose of this book is fourfold. I hope to help us

1. subjectify those we've objectified,

2. empathize with those we've vilified,

3. humanize those we've deified, and

4. see that our posture is just as important as our position.

I want to show you how in everything you say and everything you do, your posture can be one of love. No matter your viewpoint, you can stay in love when you disagree. We forget that even when our positions are clear, our intentions sound, and our arguments foolproof, if our postures are crooked, it won't matter much in the end. We won't be heard. "If I speak in the tongues of men and of angels, but have not love, I am a noisy gong or a clanging cymbal" (1 Corinthians 13:1). We can make a great point, but if we don't make it out of love for the other person, then it will often pierce and wound like a spear, not momentarily sting like a healing swab. Our great argument won't make nearly as much difference as we hoped it would. If it does, it will be in the wrong direction.

Have you noticed—especially in these past few electric years— that if you force your view on someone else, they're only more likely to dig in their heels or run for the hills? In the pages that follow, I might not effectively change your position on some things, but I do hope I can help you reconsider your posture.

Because true worshippers will worship in spirit and truth.

That is to say, truth without love isn't truth.

Love without truth isn't love.

I want to be honest on all these pages. I'm aware that my viewpoint, as an American male musician who is Protestant and white, comes from a distinctly privileged position. My ability to elegantly disagree begins when I acknowledge my own boxes and biases. We all have them; we just might not recognize them yet. I do stress *yet*. I don't know what led you to pick up this book, but I can tell you why I've written it. I want to love more, listen more compassionately, and never stop learning—which I hope you will be inspired to do as well.

And the good news? There's room for both of us in the gray.

GRACE
IN THE
GRAY

1

Leaning In

I've never learned anything while I was talking.

—Larry King

My sister once stabbed me in the arm with a pencil. I still bear the mark. If you look just above my right elbow, you'll see a little faded gray circle of lead just beneath the surface of my skin. I'm not trying to paint my sister in some villainous light. The truth is, I deserved it.

I forget what we were arguing about, but I know I had spent the better part of an hour harnessing all the agitative force I could muster to see just how angry I could make her. After enduring my assaults for longer than I had expected any human being to last, she slowly turned her gaze in my direction. With one glance at the wild look in her eye, I recoiled. She made two moves simultaneously. In a flash, she grabbed her mechanical pencil and lunged at me with all her might. I shot away from the table and was able to elude her reach for four or five sprints around the kitchen. She maniacally waved the pencil over her head and screamed, "I DON'T WANT TO HEAR ANY MORE!"

I slipped as I turned the corner to traverse the staircase. Seizing her advantage, she dove and plunged her writing tool deep into my right biceps. It dangled from my arm for a few moments before falling to the floor. I turned white with shock and finally yelled, "YOU STABBED ME! I CAN'T BELIEVE YOU JUST STABBED ME!"

She did not respond immediately. Rather, she stood up silently, smoothed her wrinkled top, and collected herself. Then, with a casual toss of her hair, she said, "Well, now you'll think twice before you aggravate me."

She was right. We didn't fight much after that.

I understand not everyone has lead buried in their upper arm from a childhood grievance, but I do know we all carry scars from the disagreements we've encountered throughout our lives. Anecdotal evidence suggests we could all use a couple of lessons on how to handle confrontation.

How do I know? Well, everyone who's heard me explain the premise of this book has chuckled and said, "Oh yeah, I'd like to read a book on that. I think the world could use a little more grace right now." While maybe some were just being kind (*thanks, Mom*), I think most meant it. The world could always use a bit more mercy. What if we learned to lean in instead of lunge at one another?

You just proved it too. The fact that you're reading this likely means you've had fights of your own. You wouldn't read a book on the subject if you didn't sense your need for it. Let me encourage you—if you're interested in learning how to disagree in a more loving way, you may not feel it just yet, but change is possible. You proved it by opening this book. Great job. You're already on your way. In the following pages, I hope I can help you find a way to lay your pencils down and learn a more elegant way to disagree.

Here's the hardest part. Before we do anything else, we must learn the art of making room by leaning in. If we are to love in the gray spaces—the places where our arguments find justified footing on either side—curiosity and kindness must lead the way. Our desire to be heard must not overpower our need to hear what others are saying. Our desire to be understood must not overshadow our need to understand others.

But how on earth do we do that? When you feel unheard in an argument, it feels excruciating to shut up and listen. How do you lean in when the other party is already lunging? But as I heard during an interview with the great Jeff Goldblum on the YouTube series *Hot Ones* (while he was eating an assortment of increasingly spicy vegan hot wings), Goldblum's acting teacher Sandy Meisner once quipped, "You're only interesting to the extent that you're interested."[1] That might not make sense, so let me unpack it. I think the world would be a better place if we were all a little more like Jeff Goldblum's acting teacher. By that, I mean that when someone is sitting across the aisle from me and they're showing no signs of caring about my perspective, I want to learn to lean in with curiosity rather than demand they pay attention to the brilliance of my argument.

That is the heart of this book. I want to cultivate interest and fascination. Everyone wants to be interesting and fascinating, but those characteristics begin to show up only as a by-product of learning to be interested and fascinated. I want to cultivate a "tell me more" posture. I may win fewer arguments, but I might just learn a thing or two about the other person—and about myself—if I talk a little less and listen a little more. If you're on board with that aim, if you share that simple desire, let me explain to you how I got there.

RELATIONSHIPS CAN BE LES MISÉRABLES

As I've already alluded to with my pencil-stab story, my upbringing had a bent toward controversy. I'd like to think our parents instilled a deep sense of justice in us at an early age, but for whatever reason, we Doneheys love a good row. My family will sit around a Thanksgiving table for hours "discussing" everything from foreign policy to the best movies of the year. I say "discussing" because the first Thanksgiving my wife spent with my family, she had to retreat to the bedroom on several occasions.

"Why does your family get so angry?" she croaked out between tears.

"Who's angry?" I answered, a bit too emphatically.

Looking back, it's funny now. I was a bit like a frog in a pot of water. I was so used to the heat that I didn't even notice when the atmosphere might be boiling for someone else who was just getting dumped into the pot. I had no idea every family didn't operate like mine. I am pleased to say, we've matured a lot in this area. I'd even say, though we are a tempestuous lot, we don't carry around many hidden grievances. You don't have to wonder where you stand. But the point is, I grew up learning to argue. I guess you could say it was part of our culture at large and my family culture specifically. We never shied away from a good old-fashioned tussle.

Knowing that I was brought up in that environment, you can understand why it's taken me most of my adult life to learn to appreciate the viewpoint of someone who doesn't see things my way. It's been a whole new art form to learn how to lean in with grace extended instead of jump in with weapons wielded. In my early years, if I couldn't win someone over to my position, I would either assume they were an ambassador of Satan or dismiss them as needing medication. Let's say I didn't exactly possess the gift of inviting criticism or of giving grace. Sometimes I'd rage. Sometimes I'd deflate. Whatever the result, I couldn't stand walking away when things ended in disagreement. In my mind, things were always black or white. Mystery was not an option. There had to be a clear winner and a loser, and that's just the way it was.

What's worse, when a heated conversation would stall, I used to antagonize my opponent until they climbed back into the ring with me. Remember exhibit A, "The Pencil Story"? There was no quitting on me. I'd pester until the tension found traction again. And if agitation failed, I'd switch tactics. If I thought my challenger was wriggling their way out before the fight concluded, I would simply dial up my passion. I found early on that when logic fails, escalation is a simple ploy to keep things interesting. If I couldn't be convincing, I would be loud. The problem with getting louder is that it's often the opposite of leaning in. No one leans toward someone who's shouting. We wince. We pull back. Offense leads to defense, and the battle continues.

Looking back, the louder I got, the more I trapped myself in my own perspective and pushed away the very person I was trying to pull in. Have you experienced what I'm talking about? You get louder in volume and greater in tenacity, and then suddenly everyone else gets a bit more muffled. Cultivating an atmosphere of curiosity will help expose our uninspected tendencies. For instance, if you yell at a football game, no one will notice the noise. But try shouting at that same volume in a library. Every head will turn in alarm.

What helped change my ways? To put it simply, grace happened. And when it did, the space around me got quieter. It started in the tenth grade while I was reading *Les Misérables* for Mrs. Raney's English class. I had just read the famous scene where the bishop gives the candlesticks to Jean Valjean. Although lesser known, the *next* scene is what began my great unraveling. If you're unfamiliar with it, let me summarize it for you: A young boy, Petit Gervais, comes walking down the path, flipping some coins. He's having a great day, skipping and singing to himself, until he accidentally drops his most valuable coin at Valjean's feet. The convict proceeds to step on it, intending to keep it for himself. The boy marches down the path, straight up to Valjean, screaming and begging for his coin back. Valjean doesn't move. The boy runs off crying while Valjean is left to wonder at his own cruelty. Coming to his senses, he runs after Gervais to return the coin, but it's too late. Valjean runs, screaming for the boy, but cannot find him. Eventually, he collapses with exhaustion, and then for the first time in nineteen years, Jean Valjean weeps. Victor Hugo, the author, writes a few lines here that I think are worth sharing with you:

> To this celestial kindness he opposed pride, which is the fortress of evil within us. He was indistinctly conscious that the pardon of this priest was the greatest assault and the most formidable attack which had moved him yet; that his obduracy was finally settled if he resisted this clemency; that if he yielded, he should be obliged to renounce that hatred with which the actions of other men had filled his soul through so many years, and which pleased him; that this time it was necessary to conquer or to be conquered; and that a struggle, a colossal and final struggle, had been begun between his viciousness and the goodness of that man.[2]

All right, as a twenty-first-century reader, you might not have been expecting words like *clemency* and *obduracy*. Don't feel bad. I had to look them up too. Let me explain this part of the story. In one moment, Valjean was overcome with the reality that receiving the bishop's kindness was "the greatest assault and the most formidable attack" he had ever experienced. Why? Well, he realized that either he must let mercy melt the hardness of his heart or his heart would be hardened forever. "To conquer or to be conquered," as Hugo stated.

I don't know why, but as a sixteen-year-old kid, those words indelibly changed me. I realized that I had been doing a lot of conquering but maybe I needed to let myself be conquered. I don't think enough people consider that when they talk about wanting grace. If you want undeserved merit for yourself, you must then desire that for everyone. Otherwise, you haven't received grace at all, have you? To be forgiven, we have to let our egos lose. We have to lose our right to lord over others as well. We have to let go of earning grace altogether. As Dallas Willard said, "Grace is not opposed to effort, it is opposed to earning."[3] Grace was a surrender I hadn't experienced before, but when it began to make its way into my operating system, I started living under a whole new paradigm. For me, this was the beginning of finding a more loving way to disagree.

GRACE PARADIGM

A lot of us haven't converted to a grace paradigm, and it shows in the way we handle conflict. If you keep resisting mercy for yourself, be assured you won't have any left for anyone else. Are you still in that place? Are you still living like Jean Valjean, deciding whether or not you'll give in to grace? Are you converting to a way of grace, or are you still living life in the quid-pro-quo, antiquated eye-for-an-eye system of merciless living? I've got to warn you, friend: There's no peace waiting for you there. When we live that way, we almost always go through most of our lives bouncing between the poles of defensiveness and defeat. It's endless and exhausting. It certainly doesn't help us more lovingly lean in with the people around us. I know this only because I still struggle with jumping to those default settings every day. The ping-pong oscillation of defense and defeat only ever leaves me worn out and alone. Believe me when I tell you, that system is broken.

Reading *Les Misérables* in my tenth-grade literature class changed me. I saw that I needed mercy and that everyone else needed it too.

It changed the way I talked to God.

It changed the way I talked to people.

It changed the way I interacted with everyone.

I stopped stepping on coins. I started giving them away.

I finally stopped shouting and began leaning in to listen.

I didn't have to scrounge and claw and hoard for myself. There was suddenly enough grace to go around.

Or maybe I should say, it is *still* changing the way I interact with others. That's a bit more vulnerable, and it's certainly more true. I'm still learning and relearning how to let grace have its way in me. You can call it justification or sanctification; I call it the great rewiring. Sure, my old system still flares up plenty of times during conflict. My cheeks get hot. My heart races. My palms still sweat when I'm challenged on my opinions. But now my heart and mind seem to eventually override my body and extend grace.

There's a new system at work. It is working. I hope this book helps you do the same.

I've heard of grace-based parenting; imagine grace-based arguing. I think it's possible. You might be thinking, *How does that help with inviting disagreement, though? And why all this grace talk? Just get to the point where I can learn how to win an argument, Mike.* Well, this is not that kind of book. I'm starting with a personal experience with grace because I truly believe we'll never learn to graciously converse with others until that wound is first addressed in our own hearts. When grace is our baseline, being disapproved of no longer feels like being disowned. We can even invite divergence because we know where we stand. We know whose love we stand in.

Think this through with me. If I'm accepted by God and so are you, then our utmost priority is to believe it and help others believe it. Every argument I engage in is subservient to that aim. I don't need to be as concerned with letting others know I'm right as much as letting them know they're loved. Now, I know truth and love go hand in hand, but let's be honest here. How often are we really concerned about loving others with the truth we're sharing? Put simply, grace makes us better listeners because it helps clear out the condemning voices in our own heads. The space left behind makes discourse possible.

DISAGREEMENT IS HEALTHY

How differently would your conversations go if you knew your ultimate purpose was to love the other person? You might find yourself being okay with being wrong. You might even be okay when you're misunderstood or the other person disagrees with you. That's a wild idea for many of us. We tend to believe that a lot of disagreement is the mark of something dysfunctional in our relationships. Lately I'm realizing it's a sign that something is actually healthy about them. Check out the Psalms sometime, and marvel at what it looks and sounds like for David, a man after God's own heart, to be in relationship with the Divine. He's constantly lamenting, moaning, and questioning. That's incredibly intriguing to me. God even calls His chosen people *Israel*, which means "wrestles with God." Maybe healthy relationships with God and people are built not on reluctant compliance but on a mutual trust that makes space for us to vent and work through it all.

I'm learning that when everyone in my life agrees with me 100 percent of the time, chances are I'm not really in a relationship with anyone but myself. It's the same with the Lord. If the God I pray to never refutes me, then chances are I'm actually praying to a God I've fashioned in my own image. If the God I pray to always agrees with me, then I'm probably just praying to myself.

Human relationships are tricky, though. Obviously, God can handle all my questions and blunders. He's God. He really has seen and heard it all. Humans, however, aren't usually quite as merciful as the God of the universe. To see disagreement in human relationships as a sign of health takes a significant amount of reframing. You could even say it's counterintuitive to what makes a relationship in the first place. We tend to get in *relationship* with those whom we *relate* to. It's at the heart of the word. Friendships are formed by relating over similar interests. We bond over the things we have in common. But is it possible to find connection in the places where we dissent?

STAYING IN LOVE

Staying in love with my wife has taught me more about this subject than any argument I've ever been in. Romance usually begins with agreement, not conflict. It starts with that shared feeling, that realization of sameness. We connect over quickening pulses and widening eyes. We tend to fall in love with someone based on everything we hold in common. All those relatable qualities are what draw us in. We can't believe it. *"Wait, you like that movie too? Wait, I thought I was the only person who laughed at that. That's your favorite restaurant? I love that place! Incredible!"* Similarities kindle romance. The power of a shared glance lights us ablaze. Sparks fly when we realize we're not alone and someone else sees the way we do.

But anyone who's been in a relationship for any considerable amount of time will tell you that there's a massive difference between *falling* in love and *staying* in love. Falling in love is easy. It's agreement after agreement. But the art of staying in love is learning to love the places we disagree. To stay in love, we must relate in all the ways in which we're different. This is no small effort. Staying in love requires cultivating your appreciation for the other in all the little ways that person confounds and mystifies you. Simply put, we fall in love with our own reflection. We stay in love by truly taking in and beholding the other.

I had a friend once tell me that we fall in love with our similarities but we stay in love by learning to love each other's differences. We say, "Wow! You like curling? Fascinating. It seems strange and boring to me." "I didn't know sponging was a sport. Tell me why you love it." It's incredible how much wonder we can experience if we simply learn to listen more and talk less. We make room when we lean in. Thanks to my wife, I've learned that appreciating dissent in my relationships looks a lot like learning to stay in love.

The chapters that follow capture my journey of learning to look for that mystery in all my relationships. I want to learn how to keep leaning in. Don't you? I want to engage in discussion more lovingly because I'm learning to appreciate someone else's views, even if I think they're crazy. Who knows, they might learn to love me in the places I'm a little crazy too.

2

Surprised by Song

Music is the shorthand of emotion.

—Leo Tolstoy

Y ou might be thinking, *Loving others sounds lovely. I'd love to find beauty in the gray. I'd love to learn how to disagree more lovingly. I've been trying to lean in. It's why I'm reading this book. I'm in. But . . . I just don't understand why a musician thinks he knows more about it than the next guy. What makes you think you're uniquely wired to write on the subject, Mike?*

This is a fair question. I want to answer it by turning your attention to the miraculous mystery we call music. Falling in love with music was my next great step in finding grace in the gray. What Victor Hugo started, music drove home.

MUSIC: MADDENINGLY, MAGICALLY SUBJECTIVE

If there's one thing that isn't black and white, it's music. Even in college, you can't study music *fact;* you can study only music *theory.* Music is, in its essence, a mystery to study, not a problem to be solved. Doesn't that sound familiar? I suppose music is a lot like relationships.

Like our interpersonal connections, music is both incredibly mysterious and bafflingly subjective. I would even go so far as to say it's *annoyingly* subjective. Think about the last argument you had over a band you love but someone else despises. It can be downright comical when you find you can't succinctly defend your reasoning for liking whatever group it is. It's especially hilarious if the person you're engaged with has some real classical training or expertise. Eventually you find yourself saying, "You know, you may not like that band, but really what exasperates you the most is that other people *do.* And you know what, as much as you know about it, those other people are still not wrong." This person might still try to convince you otherwise with a tirade on musical composition, but you'll simply say, "Yeah, but I like it." It's like trying to convince someone their taste buds should be different. It's like the time I tried to make some high-end pour-over coffee for my cousin who at the end of the taste test still preferred his Folgers Black Gold. You're left wondering how they could be so wrong. But they're not wrong, and neither are you. That's the beautiful problem with music.

Music is a space between.

It's a thin place, of sorts, where the physical and spiritual dance. It's where the line between earth and heaven blur. Music accesses emotions we didn't know we could feel. Spirit and body collide when a song begins. The next time you're at a concert, look around the arena at the start of the song everyone has been waiting for. It's like the wind: You can't see it, but you see its effects.

Music makes us time travelers.

Music can pull us to the past and push us into the future. In an instant, we can be transported back in time to our car in high school, to our wedding day, to any number of triumphs and tragedies scattered throughout our lives. It can also make us whimsical, throwing us into a headspace of dreaming a thousand futures yet to unfold. Cue *The Greatest Showman*. Music—maybe more than any other thing I've encountered in my life—is the grayest and most beautiful of spaces.

Music saved my life.

If you've read my first book, *Finding God's Life for My Will*, you already know this story, but here's a quick recap if you haven't. I suffered a near-death accident in high school. Learning to play the guitar carried me through the healing process. I could even say that I owe my life to music. God used it to carve a path for me I couldn't have imagined for myself. "Music," as Tolstoy said, "is the shorthand of emotion." It cuts to the quick. It has power to move the heart in the shortest amount of time. It's a soul-exploring shortcut. Even though we understand it to some degree, music remains far more wondrous than we could ever put into words.

Music illuminates.

Songs have the ability to say what we wanted to but couldn't. How many times have you thought, *That's exactly what I was feeling; I just couldn't find the words*? To me, the union of lyric and melody is one of the most fascinating relationships in the universe. I'll never quite comprehend why a phrase that is sung carries a weight that isn't possible in plain speech.

These mysteries are just some of the reasons I've given my life to songwriting for more than twenty years. I never feel more enraptured or more at home than when a song is born out of thin air. I might be taking it too far here, but it's like stepping through the veil to the other side. It's like peeling back layer after layer of your thoughts and feelings until you're left naked and trembling in awe of discovering some timeless truth you never knew was always there. I know several songwriters who say they don't need to go to therapy anymore because they find healing in every writing session. I also know writers who started to go to therapy because of the things their songs were teaching them. Learning to write songs has taught me more about my own soul than any other practice has. It has also taught me more about the allure of gracious discord than any other practice I've engaged. Learning to co-write songs has taken me even deeper into finding grace in the gray. Co-writing often initially feels more like demolition than architecture, but it's incredible to see what kind of song gets built up when you give someone permission to pick it apart and tear it down. There are certain songs I have had the privilege of co-writing that I'm sure I never could have written on my own. In short, songwriting has shown me the value of disagreement.

CO-WRITING IS EGO EXPOSURE

I'll never forget the first time I tried co-writing a song, more than twenty years ago. I had been in a band with another songwriter, Drew, for years, so you would think we would have tried writing together by that point. But instead, he and I merely traded songs back and forth.

"Here's another one!" I would say as I rushed through it. "Do you like it?"

"Sure," Drew would answer flatly. "It's fine."

He might suggest changing some of my rudimentary chord choices, but other than that, we left each other's songs alone. Saying "I like it" or "It's fine" was usually the totality of our criticism. Deep down, I think we were both too scared or too proud to expose our egos to someone else's opinion. It didn't need to be that way. We could have invited each other's subjectivity into our creative process, but at that point, our art was still too precious to us to do so.

Then Michael Neale showed up.

I was working at a church called Christ Fellowship in Palm Beach Gardens, Florida. I was playing a lot of music in a lot of services for a lot of people. However, I wasn't publicly playing anything I wrote. I was playing other people's songs. (Looking back, it's funny to realize how much church worship can feel like a massive spiritual karaoke party.) As much as I wanted to write and sing my own compositions, I found that coordinating music and services for young adult, college, and high school gatherings took all my time and kept me racing.

At this point, I was very much a novice songwriter. Most of my ideas were mostly terrible. I'm sure that's why Drew didn't comment often. He probably didn't know where to start. I've heard it said that you have to write a hundred bad songs before you can write a good one. I think for me it might have been a thousand. I didn't dare play them in a service at church, but I did start playing them for my kinder friends who would indulge me by listening. No one ever gave me any feedback. They would just smile and endure my songs to the end. Usually, an awkward silence would follow. Then they would ask if I knew any Chris Tomlin songs.

Well, Michael Neale was the Chris Tomlin of my church. By

that, I mean he was a huge deal. The guy had record deals. *Record deals!* He was our local top dog who had moved to Nashville and come back to share his glory with the rest of us amateur-hour underlings. He was writing songs and facilitating musical worship for the "big church," as we lovingly referred to it.

One day, Mr. Neale called a meeting of us student ministry minions. "Bring the best song idea you're working on, and we will critique each other."

I remember a chill running down my spine. "Critique?" I started sweating. "What do you mean, Michael? You mean, like, tell each other how much we like it?"

"Sure," he replied from behind his blue-tinted shades. "We'll talk about *if* we like it. We'll give each other ideas on what's good and what we would change."

"Oh," I said, a bit confused. *Change.* I rolled the word around in my head for a minute, not sure what he meant. "Sure, sure. Sounds cool," I lied. It did not sound cool. It sounded painful.

And it was.

A few weeks later, the other student worship team feeders* and I made the trek between buildings. Even though we worked in the youth building, we had to be invited into the main auditorium. A janitor met us outside and scanned us in. It felt like sneaking into Santa's workshop. We were dazzled by the size of the stage and the grand expanse of the empty seats. This was the big dance. We knew we had a lot to learn.

Michael popped his head out from backstage and called us over. "This way, guys! Bring your guitars!" The seven of us awk-

---

* In *Finding God's Life for My Will,* I explain in detail why I avoid using the term *leader.* The short version is that Jesus didn't call Peter to "lead" the church but "feed" it.

wardly filed in behind the curtain and made our way through the lighting equipment and fog machines sitting on the floor. We finally found a circle of plushy chairs arranged and waiting for us in the choir room. We sat down and stared at one another uncomfortably. It was dead quiet. We didn't move. We barely breathed.

Michael finally broke the ice. "All right, guys. I'll go first. Here's a fun song I wrote about an underwater fish party."

"What?" I coughed out accidentally. "You wrote a song about what?"

"Oh, yeah," Michael replied nonchalantly. "Even if you're writing worship tunes, you've got to get every idea out. You have to see how far the rabbit hole goes."

His words shocked me. I had perceived Michael as a bit of a saint. I thought he must get melodies beamed down to his brain straight from on high. To be in the sacred music space, he had to be holier than the rest of us. I definitely didn't think he'd be wasting his holy time on songs about dancing sea life.

I suddenly felt more relaxed and even more perplexed.

His song was fun. I don't remember much more about it than that. But what I do recall is how excited he was to get our feedback. It stunned me. He wanted to know what could be different. Where was the melody feeling right? What chords could shift? What would be a better way to say it? Remember, I had never dared to even consider editing my songs before. I certainly didn't imagine editing someone else's.

Emboldened, I volunteered to play one next. I had what I thought was a pretty good start to a song. In fact, my friend Adam had heard the chorus and wanted me to play it at his wedding the following month. I think it was the first time anyone had ever heard a song I wrote and asked to hear it again. I was amped to usher in my friend's matrimony with an original song, but there was a problem: It wasn't finished. Maybe this opportunity with Michael would help me break through the writing blocks I had encountered trying to finish it. With a deep breath, I offered what I had so far to the group.

Michael was the first to speak up. "You know, I actually really like the chorus."

I already didn't like how he used the word *actually*. Worse, I could feel a big old *but* coming.

"But . . ." He mused for a moment. "Your pre-chorus comes out of nowhere. You're talking about a bride and how she's the love of your life, and then you suddenly say, 'You've been running away from me.' It doesn't make sense. You'll need to address the tension there so the listener knows what's coming."

I'm so glad he couldn't read my thoughts: *What! How dare you!*

A sudden taste of bile crept into my mouth. *Who do you think you are, anyway, Mr. Neale? Do you not know that I've already been commissioned to play this song at a wedding? If it's good enough for someone's covenantal vows, I think it's plenty good enough for anyone else listening. I can't believe you would offer up such paltry polish for my already glimmering work. This song is gold. Gold, I tell you!*

Despite my initial revulsion, the biggest problem with Michael's assessment of my song was that he was absolutely correct. That was why I played the song for the group. I knew it wasn't as good as it could be; I just didn't want to admit that I needed anyone's help to get it there. I marinated in his comments for a week after our meeting and finally succumbed to his suggestions. I changed the words. The final product was a song called "Beloved," and it went on to make my band's first national release, *Over and Underneath*. What's funny is that if I hadn't listened to his analysis, I would have shortchanged the final product. It needed someone else's ears to hear where it could go.

I didn't realize it at the time, but I was getting to develop an annoying little muscle called humility.

Almost twenty years and thousands of songwriting sessions later, I'm getting used to the disappointment of having the melodies and lyrics I've slaved over casually dismissed in seconds. I've learned to keep coming back for more. "Oh, you don't like that piece of my soul? Here's another one. Oh, you don't like that piece either? Here's another one." On and on it goes. Songwriting is not for the faint of heart.

For me, co-writing matured my writing faster than plugging away on my own. Some folks need solitude to work on their art, but I realized I was working that way mostly because it was safe and predictable. It wasn't until I started co-writing that I really began to develop as a songwriter. The speed and veracity of feedback let you build your writing muscles twice as fast—or so it seems. If you've never co-written a song before, I'll just say this: *You won't make headway until you get used to being critiqued.* You learn quickly that when you co-write a song, you can't hold your ideas precious. You've got to kick the Sméagol out of the room. You've got to let the other person shoot your ideas down. Or in some cases, set a dumpster fire to them.

Learning to grow thick skin can be painful, but it's worth it every time that outside voice helps an idea click or lets you know what resonates. It's also so rewarding when your co-writer's face suddenly brightens and you look at each other like paleontologists in the Badlands who've just found the first claw of what will eventually turn out to be an entire fossilized dinosaur. Songwriting is like brushing away the dirt one sweep at a time. If the fossil is the song, the dirt is often my ego. Co-writing, then, is like having a team helping on the dig. It hurts more—all those hands brushing away at the crust of my pride—but it sure is faster. You might not see the benefit of several hands digging at once while it's happening. But once you stand back and see what's been exposed, you realize something has been unearthed that is far greater than you could have imagined on your own.

There are a few things songwriters are forced to learn quickly: Sometimes your idea is terrible. Sometimes you need help with the crafting. *Sometimes being corrected is the best thing that could ever happen to you.*

I'm finally finding there's a slow but necessary separation where my worth and my production are no longer inextricably intertwined. Having so many ideas shot down and others celebrated is teaching me something important: *I am neither my mistakes nor my successes. I am not my bad ideas or my good ones.* And when I finally understand this deep down in my psyche, something incredible happens. I not only handle correction, but I also begin to actively seek it out. I want to see where I got it wrong because I want to learn. I stop running away from correction and instead desire to receive it.

This knowledge transcends music. For example, when my editor, Susan, sent edits back on the original draft of my first book, I could hear her hesitancy in telling me I had improvements to make: "We have quite a few recommended revisions and comments. But remember these are just suggestions."

I shot back, "Oh, don't worry. Bring it on! My ideas aren't precious anymore. I need you to help me make them better." She marveled at the way I was able to process feedback—all thanks to Michael Neale, I suppose. Music taught me that just because my idea is wrong, it doesn't mean I'm wrong.

A BAND IS A MARRIAGE

It's difficult to quantify how many ways music has helped me find grace in the gray. Music has forced me to learn how to disagree with others in ways I might not have been able to achieve otherwise. While co-writing taught me how to lay down my ego and work with fellow songwriter paleontologists, learning to cooperate in a band forced me to resolve conflict and deal with tensions that I otherwise would have simply walked away from.

Anyone who's ever been in a band can tell you that bandmates are forced to deal with things more quickly than others might. In other occupations, you can often delay resolution. Let's say you have a tiff with a co-worker. In most work environments, you could clock out at the end of the day and try your best to avoid them around the office for the next few weeks. That doesn't work if your co-worker is onstage with you every day and sleeping next to you on the floor of the van every night. Sheer proximity forces your hand at conflict resolution.

It's more than a job. Being in a band is a lot like being in a marriage—with four other people. If you don't work out your relational quandaries, you're in for a bumpy ride. If you're married, imagine multiplying your conflict quota times four. And if your bandmates are all married, then you get to experience a multiple of eight. That's a lot of people to be married to.

In a band, the need to see someone else's perspective is endless. You're trying to make not only art together but a living too. That means you have everyone's livelihood to consider, as well as their opinions. Throw in living in a van or on a bus together and the possibilities for discord are limitless. I can't tell you how many arguments we had over who left a mess in the common area. Whether it's bus life, deciding what tour you should go on, what your album artwork should look like, the length of the song's intro, or what the guitar part should be, opportunities to disagree are everywhere. And that's just with the bandmates. Now throw opinions of management and label executives and crew members and promoters and fans into the mix and you can imagine the combustions waiting at every turn.

I was in my band, Tenth Avenue North, for twenty-one years. No other experience in my life has taught me more about loving the people you're in constant disagreement with. My band taught me that everyone sees the world in wildly different colors. Having others describe what they see when it doesn't line up with what I see doesn't minimize my vision—it expands it. My band taught me how to forgive because we couldn't let conflict fester even for a moment. My band taught me how to talk to people. I can't tell you how many epic throwdowns we had over the silliest things. We had group feelings time, Enneagram study circles, and endless discussions on conspiracy theories and best coffee-making techniques. We had to learn to speak one another's languages or we were never going to make something like harmony.

People ask me what kind of music we made. The easiest way to describe it is to call us a contemporary Christian music (CCM) band, which truthfully, isn't my favorite of descriptions but helps gives some context. (In no way am I ashamed to let people know I make music about Jesus; it's just I think the word *Christian* is better suited as a noun rather than an adjective.)

The lyrical content was of a spiritual nature. My lyrics still are. And for the last twenty years, they've been a doorway leading me into ten lifetimes' worth of conflicting viewpoints and awkward conversations on just about everything. Not only have I worked in several churches, but I've also played concerts in more than a thousand different churches, encompassing almost as many differ-ent denominational circles. I've certainly had to learn the art of navigating relational and spiritual contention.

Something about my being onstage seems to generate a lot of interest in my opinion about certain things. I feel pressure when that happens, and being in a band labeled as Christian seems to double the burden. I've warned many young CCM artists starting out, "Whether you like it or not, fans will come to view you as musical pastors. You can dismiss it or accept it. They're looking to you as some kind of spiritual authority." It took me a long time to accept that people were looking at me that way.

I think I let a lot of people down.

Maybe it was because we released songs about confessing se-crets. Or maybe it was because we released an album called *The Struggle*. Or I guess it could have been an EP we put out about *The Things We've Been Afraid to Say*. Whatever the reason, throughout those years my social media inboxes were filled with hundreds, maybe even thousands, of messages that were eerily similar. Every message had a different name and described a slightly different circumstance, but they all seemed to tell the same story— something like this:

> *I tried it. This whole "light meets the dark" thing. I tried con-fessing my dark and dirty secrets. But I wasn't met with the grace you talked about. I was met with resistance . . . with dis-gust. I was kicked out of my church. I was disowned by my family. I wasn't met with mercy. Instead of saying "Ohhhh," they went, "Ewww." I was left to my own devices. I was given the cold shoulder when I was desperate for embrace. And now, I don't have any idea where to go.*

Not only that, but anytime I put a toe in the water near anything remotely controversial, the pistols were drawn:

I can't believe you read Harry Potter! How dare you drink wine! Your music is straight from the devil. I can't believe you would admit to being tempted. I'm burning all of your music. How dare you not message me back! You claim to love Jesus; now I know you're a fraud.

Unfortunately, when someone sees you as a spiritual authority, you're going to get credit for things God did and you're going to come under fire for anything you didn't do right. That responsibility is a lot to shoulder.

After being in this role for as long as I have, I've made my fair share of mistakes. My bandmates can tell you that. But I've also gained insight and learned a lot of lessons. The greatest lesson I've learned is that most of us actually agree on much more than we think. You'd be shocked by how many essentials we have in common. I've also learned that, unfortunately, we all love to let the little things balloon into big things. I think music has helped me learn the art of de-escalation. It's taught me to dance instead of doubling down. Yes, there's a time for truth, but there's also a time to two-step. In the pages ahead, I'll be sharing some of the stories, mindsets, and practices that have helped shape the way I move through the world. I hope you'll find them helpful. I hope they help you have more grace in the gray spaces and more hope for the disagreements that can feel so painful in the moment. I hope I can help us move to the rhythm of grace. Maybe in the pages ahead, we can learn to tread more lightly. Everyone is indeed fighting a hard battle.

Get the Fork Out of Here

Never let bitterness make a home in your heart; raise the rent and kick it out.

—Matshona Dhliwayo

The reason I find myself so passionately disagreeing with others isn't always that something is wrong "out there." More times than I care to admit, the reason I make enemies out of dissenters is that I've got my own unaddressed dysfunction. I know this because whenever I've asked God to change someone else's mind, He's tended to kindly respond, "Well, let's start with you changing the way you view that person instead."

God has a way of calling me out.

I don't like to think that Jesus is using the people I'm frustrated with to teach me more about myself. But that's kind of His thing, isn't it? I grew up hearing that if I prayed for patience, God would "bless me" with trying circumstances that would give me the opportunity to grow in it. It turns out, when I pray to be more gracious, God allows people in my life who will require more grace for me to love.

It's annoying.

It's genius.

If you're going to learn patience, you're going to have to wait. If you're going to learn graciousness, you're going to have to forgive. If you're going to welcome criticism, you must first deal with your own inner critic. If you want to get healthy, you don't change everyone else's diet; you change your own. Maybe that's how disagreement works. Maybe the problem isn't out there but in here. What goes in is what comes out, right? That's why I started drinking smoothies. Even though a smoothie almost killed me.

DEATH BY SMOOTHIE

They say a smoothie can be one of the most nutrient-dense substances a human can consume. The ability to consume large amounts of shrubbery, vitamin powder, and protein at once is truly amazing. If you haven't ever started your morning with a delicious, blended, protein-packed infusion of ice cream–like goodness, I suggest you try it. I've been in the smoothie game since early 2008, back when I was working on my wedding-day LGNB. (That stands for "look good naked body," in case you didn't know.)

The LGNB must have worked because I now have four daughters. Like most kids I've met, they hate nutrients in their food. If it were up to them, they would eat only candy and pizza, and all things the color brown. If they chose the menu, they'd plow through nothing but french fries seasoned with Fun Dip and would undoubtedly slip into a sugar-induced coma in three days' time.

But, praise the Lord, I found an exception. They, too, love

smoothies. Granted, we differ in the kinds of smoothie we will ingest. I honestly don't care what a smoothie tastes like. In fact, the worse it tastes, the more I trust it. I don't view the smoothie as a culinary masterpiece meant to delight my taste buds. I view "the smooth" as a vehicle for efficient vitamin transport. End of story. But my girls have far more sensitive palates. So, I've found that if I back off the nutrient load just a touch and double up on the palatability, I can load chocolate smoothies with plenty of nutrient-dense healthy fats and superfoods that their immature taste buds will not even detect but that will make their cellular respiration sing. (Here's a pro tip for parents wondering how to do this: Take your time. Every day, add a bit more frozen spinach than the day before. You've got to notch it up slowly.)

One morning a few months ago, I was up early preparing the aforementioned smoothies, unaware that my nine-year-old daughter had come down the stairs. I need to sidebar here for a moment to really set up the visuals for full effect. This particular child carries a special poltergeist-like quality of sliding into a room completely undetected. At that time, she also happened to have long, tangled brown curls that hung in front of her eyes, almost completely blocking her face from view. She was wearing a particularly ratty old Disney princess silk nightgown that was tattered and frayed everywhere. It had probably been washed two hundred times too many. The nightgown, together with the long hair over her eyes, gave her a look like something out of a horror movie. It was also five o'clock in the morning, and . . . did I mention she has a unique ability to ghoulishly glide into a room silent and unannounced?

I was going about my routine, creating a cold protein concoction, when I felt a presence peering down on me from the stairwell landing. I slowly turned toward the feeling until I caught sight of something hovering a few stairs up from the kitchen. I immediately stumbled backward into the cabinets and cried out to Jesus to come save me from this demon. Upon realizing it was just my daughter, I panted for a few moments and then finally garbled out, "Child! Don't do that to me."

"Sorry, Dad," she answered, unblinking and monotone. "Can I come help?"

"Yes," I said with a sigh. "Just try to dial back the Casper vibes, will you?"

She nodded in compliance before I handed her the tub of spinach, telling her to throw some in. However, I completely forgot about the avocado I had been forking in moments before. When she frightened me with her spectral presence, I dropped the avocado and the utensil into the supercharged four-hundred-horsepower Vitamix. So, my daughter threw in the spinach, which totally blocked the forgotten fork from view. I took no notice, and the two of us kept tossing ingredients in. We eventually filled the blender to the top, and I casually hit the power switch.

Armageddon ensued.

Sparks flew.

Smoke filled the kitchen.

The fork rattled violently like an angry cobra.

The lights flickered maniacally overhead as the silver snake unceasingly attacked its cage.

My daughter and I could do nothing but hold each other and scream.

The blender was clearly possessed. We kept screaming.

Suddenly, there was an explosion.

The fork burst free from its confinement, out the side of the blender, and the smoothie erupted like Mount Vesuvius. Cold green slop projected over the entire kitchen. Cascades of breakfast sludge ran down windows and dripped from the cabinets. In fact, I was still finding smoothie on the ceiling months after "the incident." I slowly emerged from my hiding place, peering over the top of the countertops and checking my stomach for holes.

BITTERNESS IS LIKE DRINKING POISON AND WAITING FOR THE OTHER PERSON TO DIE

I know this is an absurd story, but trust me, I'm going somewhere with this. I've often wondered whether bitterness isn't something like that fork—or even a sword perhaps. Being bitter is like trying to stab someone with something that must first pass through your own soul. Or, in my case, it's like trying to make a smoothie without removing the fork from the blender.

Remember how I said when I ask God to change other people, He flips the magnifying glass around? Well, bitterness is always at the top of God's script-flipping when He starts dealing with me. Why? Well, it turns out that if bitterness gets in our blenders, it will eventually ruin everything else. It doesn't matter what other practices we add to our lives. You can add workouts and meditations, charitable giving and compliments. You can add prayer time and Scripture memorization, ice baths, breathing, and thought training. But if you've got the fork of resentment down in your gears, the only way to wholeness is by extraction. Try as you might, you can't get healthy if you let bitterness remain. Sometimes health can't come through addition but subtraction. You can add every vegetable and green that has ever existed. You can add protein and complex vitamins all you want. But if you leave the fork in the blender of your heart, it's eventually going to come out sideways. And when it does, it'll blow a hole right through the center of your life.

If you want to learn how to disagree, you've got to get the fork out of there.

Here's what the apostle Paul has to say on the subject: "Do not let the sun go down while you are still angry, and do not give the devil a foothold" (Ephesians 4:26–27, NIV). The Greek word behind *foothold* is *topos*. Elsewhere throughout the New Testament, this word is translated as *place, locality,* and *opportunity.*[1] *Opportunity* is the word used in the ESV translation. Isn't that an interesting term to use? Don't give the devil an opportunity. Don't give him a chance. Don't give him a place. Don't give him a location. I think you could go further in the English and say, "Don't give the devil an inch."

As far as I can tell, the most dangerous inch of space you can give the devil is the one you give to bitterness. Most of us wouldn't think of it that way. We wouldn't think of bitterness as the fork in the blender. Growing up in church, I never would have put bitterness at the top of the "things that will keep me from being forgiven" list. I would have said "the love of money." I would have said "doing drugs," or, honestly, I probably would have said "kissing my girlfriend." I would have listed a hundred different things before I would have said "bitterness."

However, it's right there, plain as day. Right after the Lord's Prayer, Jesus lays it out. "If you forgive others their trespasses, your heavenly Father will also forgive you, but if you do not forgive others their trespasses, neither will your Father forgive your trespasses" (Matthew 6:14–15).

This is astonishing. Think about the disciples hearing this for the first time. The Jewish people were experiencing persecution. Their land had been taken from them. They were paying exorbitant taxes. They were being wrongfully and woefully ruled by Rome at that moment. Can you imagine their faces when Jesus said He wouldn't forgive the unforgiving? He didn't list any other vice here. He didn't mention anything else they might have done or experienced. He simply said, "If you withhold forgiveness from others, your Father withholds forgiveness from you" (verse 15, TPT).

Ouch, Jesus.

What on earth? What's happening here, God? I thought Your love was unconditional. So why is Jesus putting this condition on it?

As I questioned Jesus on this point, He said, "That's exactly right, Mike. The only condition I'm putting on My love is that it remains unconditional. The second you put conditions on it for someone else, you turn My love into something it isn't. The only condition to My free gift of love is that it must stay exactly that: free."

My head exploded. I stammered, "I'm too stupid to talk to You, Jesus."

Spectacular, right?

Some will say that the condition to accessing God's forgiveness is receiving it. But I'd say whoever believes it's unconditional will receive it. It's only those who put conditions on it who won't. Either we're too bad to deserve it or too good to need it. I suppose that's what trickles down to bitterness, isn't it? Either they're way worse than us, or we're too good for them. It's the same lie turned outward.

Paul says in 2 Corinthians 5:18 that we have been given the "ministry of reconciliation." I take that to mean that the reason the people of God are here on earth is to receive God's forgiveness and let others know they are forgiven. End of story.

That's our ministry.

That's what we're doing here.

We're not here to be right.

We're here to reconcile.

We're making known the story of God. How? By bearing witness to the fact that we have received His mercy. How do we do that? By offering the mercy we have received.

If that's true, then why don't I hear more about it? If unforgiveness is the one thing keeping us from forgiveness, then why aren't at least 90 percent of sermons about this? If it's the only thing that will keep Jesus from forgiving me, then I better get on that train. Before I try to deal with all my other addictions and bad habits, I ought to center the force of my will against any bitterness lurking in the recesses of my heart.

But I don't.

We don't.

In fact, we do the opposite. We justify our hurt. We justify our bitterness. This is understandable. Oftentimes, we're right to be hurt. But when we don't get curious about our hurt, when we don't learn what our hurt is trying to tell us, sometimes we end up fortifying it. Once those walls begin to go up, we tend to guard them by surrounding ourselves with people who congratulate our justification. Injury can cause us to double down. We nurse our wounds until we build an identity around them. Our offendedness feels too good to let go of. If it didn't, we wouldn't take so much offense. Yes, we'll let go of it to make amends but only after the other person apologizes first. The only thing that feels better than stroking our hurt is extending the ring to our offenders to kiss once they've adequately groveled at our feet.

Look, I'm not trying to make light of this. I know things may have happened to you that I could probably never conceive of nor understand. Maybe you have experienced unthinkable abuse. Let me encourage you. Forgiving deep hurt doesn't always happen overnight. In fact, it often takes our whole lives. But it's the horizon we point our hearts to. It's the direction we're heading. And maybe I should add, forgiving offenders doesn't necessarily mean making friends, but it will make you free. Whatever hurt you're struggling to release, I must press to convince you that the principal way strongholds take up residence in our lives is through the doorway of unforgiveness. I hear it from my good friend Jon, who counsels folks struggling with addiction. He tells me over and over that almost every client he sees might be dealing with substance abuse on the surface, but the real addiction is their unaddressed bitterness. He says it is the spring from which a river of dysfunction flows. He also says that when someone finds the grace of God to forgive, the rest of their addictions often fall like a line of dominoes.

So why don't we forgive? Why don't we see the importance of Jesus's words to us? Well, probably because our bitterness is quite justified. Some of us live lives of grand delusion, but I've found most of us don't usually struggle with unforgiveness unless we were legitimately wronged at some point. We are "right" to feel hurt, aren't we? When the other party is indeed guilty, shouldn't they be held accountable?

The short answer is yes. But while we're still waiting for an apology or for the truth to surface—while we're waiting for the darkness to be brought to light or for our offenders to come to justice this side of heaven—we must find a way to take the forks out of our blenders. Otherwise, we'll do more damage to ourselves than the initial offense did.

How do we do this? How do we lay down resentment when justice hasn't come?

MY FATHER MAILED A LETTER

My father was abused by his father. I didn't know that until I was well into my twenties. I didn't know my dad's dad, but I've been told he was verbally and physically abusive. He drank too much and hit his wife and struck my dad on multiple occasions. My dad said it got so bad at one point during high school that he bought a moped and ran away to Canada. He rode the moped from Boston to Montreal and worked at Expo 67 (the 1967 World's Fair) all summer. He said the motorbike eventually gave up the ghost and he buried it in a snowbank near the end of his time there. My dad would lay to rest the hurt he was running from, too, but that would take a few more years. After burying his bike, he eventually ran out of money and went back home.

The first chance he got, though, he joined the US Air Force and moved all the way across the country to Monterey, California, where he went to language school to train for his first assignment as a radio translator. Interestingly enough, a few decades later my band would play a concert in the same theater downtown where my father worked as a projectionist in his spare time. He wasn't in Monterey long. He was transferred to Omaha, Nebraska, where he met my mother at a party, and they quickly fell in love and *yada, yada, yada*. The story moves on.

It was maybe only five years ago that I finally thought through what my father endured at the hands of his dad. In a quickening of my spirit, I marveled that my father had never replicated the sins of his father. He had never struck me. He had never once abused me. I wondered how my dad had broken the cycle of revenge and bitterness that could have easily swept him up in its clutches.

So, I asked him. "Dad, I was just thinking. Your father was abusive, right?"

My father's usually boyish countenance darkened a shade. "Yes, that's correct," he affirmed.

"Well . . . I was wondering, How did you break the cycle? You never hit me. You never raged. I mean, you might have gone psycho on my peewee soccer referees a time or two, but I never felt like you'd ever abuse me in any way. How did you do it? How did you change your inheritance?"

My father, who never misses a chance to be grandiose, turned surprisingly somber. He spoke straight to it. "I wrote him a letter."

"Wait, what?" I questioned. I wasn't expecting him to be so quick on the draw.

"Yeah . . ." He trailed off for a moment as his eyes narrowed, thinking of how to go on. "You know, I didn't know Jesus then. Your mom and I were just married, and we started going to this church in Omaha. One Sunday the pastor said if we want to be forgiven, we must forgive. So, I was thinking about my dad, and I decided to write him a letter."

"Oooh," I said knowingly, "you wrote a letter telling your dad that you forgave him for all the things he said to you and did to you. I see."

"Wait, no," my dad interrupted. "No, it didn't say that at all, actually. In my letter, I didn't tell him that I forgave him; I asked my dad to forgive me for all the bitterness I had held in my heart toward him! I told him I loved him and that no matter what, he'd always be my dad."

"Oh," I said, bewildered by the curveball my father had just thrown at me.

"Yeah, it was the strangest thing," my dad said. "The second I put that letter in the mailbox, I felt all the weight in my world disappear from my shoulders. In fact, I don't know if he ever read my letter. He didn't need to. I was the one who needed to heal."

That still is one of the shortest and most profound exchanges I've ever had with my dad. I could hear a thousand lectures on the importance of forgiveness, but none will carry the weight of that three-minute back-and-forth with him. In a few words, I was reminded that freedom is offered to us every second if only we would be bold enough to receive it.

ETERNALLY OFFENSIVE FORGIVENESS

For my father, freedom started when he owned up to what was his to own up to. I think this is of profound importance. He might have been in the one half of a percent in the complicity department, but he embraced it wholeheartedly. He didn't look into his father's blender; he inspected his own. Since that conversation I've thought a lot about eternity and heaven—who will be there and what it will be like. I wonder whether my granddad whom I never knew will be there. I keep having this inescapable thought that I don't know if I entirely like. It might be from reading C. S. Lewis's *The Great Divorce* one too many times, but I keep having this picture of what it would be like if I was met at the pearly gates by the one person I couldn't stand.

Imagine it for a second.

You die. You ride the elevator or escalator or rainbow or whatever it is. Maybe it's the bus that Lewis describes, or maybe you appear in the blink of an eye. However you arrive, there you are, standing in front of the pearly gates. It's just like you had imagined. Peter is there. He's reading from the Book of Life, and he beams down at you as you approach. His smile is a mile wide. He reads your name with triumph. It echoes off the rubies and sapphires and diamonds. You stand tall and feel the warmth on your face. The gates begin to open, and dazzling light cascades from inside. It's blindingly white. You squint and strain your new heavenly eyes and find there's no pain. You catch a glimpse of the golden streets. You see Jesus down the road, sitting on a throne. His robe is filling the temple, and all the angels are flying around saying, "Holy, holy, holy." You knew it. It is just like you had believed. You did it. You believed in Jesus. You're in.

But then comes the dramatic hitch.

Someone is coming to meet you from behind the gates. It takes you a minute to understand the drop in your stomach. Then you realize who it is. It's that one person. It's the guy who wronged you. It's the girl who said those nasty things about you. It's that one person you couldn't stand. Maybe it's the girl who stole your boyfriend. Or even worse, maybe it's the person who took your innocence. Whoever it is, you just can't understand why you're seeing this person. They shouldn't be there. *Shouldn't they be in the other place?* Why is that one church member who kicked you out all those years ago walking toward you? And why is this person smiling—whoever they might be? The one person you thought would never be allowed in your heaven is right here, and there's no way around it. In fact, it seems like there's no other way around them since they're standing between you and the gates. You pause. You wonder whether you're in the good place after all. The person reaches out their hand and smiles. "Welcome. I'm so sorry for what I did to you. I was so wrong. Will you forgive me?" Their hand hangs there in eternity. These were the words your wounded soul so desperately longed to hear. *"I'm sorry. I was so wrong."* But you can't believe it. You won't let the words sink down into those wounds you've held so dear.

You push the person aside and make for the entrance. *Maybe in a thousand years,* you think as you spring for the gates. But Peter intercepts you. "Oh, I'm so sorry about this. I know it's a lot to take in. It is for most of us. But you see, you can't come in alone. You have to enter in pairs. Remember our triune God personifies relationship, after all, so the only way in is through. The only way we can see His face is together."

Now does that sound like heaven?

Okay, this is a dramatic hypothesis, and I admit an extrabiblical one at that. But just like Lewis's painting a picture of the nature of hell, I think this scene could help us remember the nature of heaven.

Heaven.

Who will be there? And what will be demanded of us to enter? Have you thought about the fact that your unforgiveness will need to be called out and dropped at the door? Who gets to enter the heaven you have in your head? Is there anyone you hope isn't there? May I urge you that if you don't at least hope that everyone will eventually make it there, you're in fact disagreeing with God Himself, "who desires all people to be saved and to come to the knowledge of the truth" (1 Timothy 2:4)? If anyone who comes to Jesus gets to enter, then we'd better start practicing our reconciliation skills now.

Put simply, if heaven is full of the forgiven, it is also full of those who have chosen to forgive. Heaven is full of people who receive. They receive mercy. They receive healing. They receive forgiveness for themselves and for others. They receive the grace to enter and in turn extend the invitation to others. It's why I believe one of the very last verses in Revelation is "The Spirit and the Bride say, 'Come'" (Revelation 22:17). Heaven is full of open invitation.

Hell, as the opposite, is full of those in an unforgiven state. It's why Lewis argued it's locked from the inside. It is and will be full of those who are unforgiven and unforgiving. As Lewis further surmised, "Hell . . . begins with a grumbling mood"[2] and "It's not a question of God 'sending' us to hell. In each of us there is something growing up which will of itself *be hell* unless it is nipped in the bud."[3] I think this strikes the chord quite succinctly. If heaven is real, then it will be full not only of people who disagreed with me but also of people who willfully hurt me. If I can begin to accept the fact that there will be some people next to me in eternity that I don't currently like being around, maybe it will affect how I interact with the people who so arduously disagree with me here and now. It might change the way I see the gray places. It might even help me dismantle the preciousness of my own wounds.

UNOFFENDABLE

You're probably wondering why I'm spending so much time on this message. Make no mistake. I believe *the* portal for demonic activity in our lives is bitterness. I have to believe the way demons set up shop is through the doors of resentment and unforgiveness that I leave open. That message isn't sexy, because we love to be offended. But remember, no one can ever offend you. You're the one who has to take offense. Someone else might have thrown the fork in the blender, but you're the one who is leaving it in there. Get the fork out of there.

It feels invigorating to have a one-up on someone, though, doesn't it? If I resent someone, I feel like the person owes me. And we all love to feel like we're owed something. We must ask, *Why?* Is it because deep down we know we're not enough? Is it because we know we don't match up to the original glory we were meant to have? Being owed might just help fill that need.

Grace, then, is a troubling exchange. We are freed from owing God, but simultaneously we lose the privilege of feeling owed. If heaven is an open invitation, then hell is eternal resistance. All that is required for heaven is to receive. But to receive, you have to let go of the offended-ness you're carrying in your arms.

Remember, as we grapple with how to disagree with others more lovingly, Jesus was never offended. My friend Brant wrote a great book on this singular subject. It's called *Unoffendable*.[4] In it, Brant points out that Jesus was never shocked by anyone's behavior. He never stepped back and said, "I just can't believe how bad these people are." Think about that for a moment. Jesus is never surprised by our badness. But we do see Him surprised by faith. That's something to marvel. Jesus is never shocked by my sin, but He is pleasantly surprised by my goodness. I want to stop flipping the script. It's not that I think we should be cynical, but I believe it would do us a world of good if we stopped expecting everyone to be good to us all the time. If Jesus really came into the world to save sinners, then I need to stop being flabbergasted when I run into some. I'm not owed a world of sinners treating me better than I deserve.

I'll try to be gentle here because I think this is the heart of the war we find ourselves in, but if you're deeply offended all the time, can I just ask why that might be? Why are you so surprised? If Jesus Himself could be wrongfully killed, doesn't it stand to reason we might encounter our fair share of mistreatment? In John 16:33 Jesus promised us trouble, but He also promised to be with us in it. It's good to remember that Jesus would never ask me to lay down my resentment if He hadn't. He showed us the way by crying out, "Father, forgive them, for they know not what they do" (Luke 23:34). He never asks us to do something He hasn't already done.

This is the heart of this book. If I'm going to find a new way of speaking with others, then I'm going to need a new way of seeing others. Strangely, the more readily I see others as fellow sinners in need of grace, the more readily I'll speak to them graciously. When I do, perhaps I'll understand what David was getting at when he sang, "You prepare a table before me in the presence of my enemies" (Psalm 23:5). Maybe I'm not meant to hurl my forks at my enemies. Maybe I'm meant to take the forks out so I can help set another place for them at the table.

4

Live Like I've Got No Enemies

If you want peace, you don't talk to your friends. You talk to your enemies.

—Desmond Tutu

Doesn't it sound a bit insane? Forgiveness by itself can already feel like an insurmountable task. But to take it a step further and actually set a place for our enemies at the table? Yes. I think this is what Jesus has in mind for all of us. When it comes to battling in the gray spaces, I have to believe He wants me to not only bless my enemies but stop seeing them as enemies altogether. When people who disagree with me are no longer enemies, I can look for ways to serve them instead of ways to defeat them. They are no longer obstacles to conquer; they are image bearers to bless. For many of us, this is easier said than done.

Growing up, I never had a lot of enemies, at least not that I'm aware of. When I was nine, my best friend, Nate, knocked me unconscious by dropping an ice block on my head from a tree fort. But once I woke up, I thought it was hilarious. We are still friends to this day. Sure, I would mouth off while playing sports, and even now I still feel occasional road rage, but all in all, I've gotten along pretty peaceably. My wife claims that grievances seem to slide off my back in an unusual way. Maybe that's why it's easier for me to talk about bitterness (compared with whom, I don't know because, you know, I've only ever been myself). My mom even claims that when I was a kid, I used to smile in my sleep. So, yeah, I'm not usually at sharp odds with strangers.

I haven't been in a whole lot of real danger either, for that matter. Well, I did almost die in a car accident when I was seventeen, so I suppose that's pretty dangerous. But that's not the kind of danger I'm talking about. I'm talking about being threatened. I've never been held hostage or anything. Okay, so there was the one time my friend Jon and I were mugged at knifepoint in New York City. Pardon, it wasn't a knife—we were mugged by a guy holding a box cutter. He took our wallets and ran. We found a police officer a few minutes later, who simply said, "Get in." We then got to see all of Times Square by squad car, tearing around the city while the cop kept telling us to "keep your eyes peeled" for the guy who mugged us.

And okay, now that I really think about it, there was the one time some friends and I were hunted down by an assailant with a gun. Pardon me while I digress yet again. We were minding our own business, hanging out in the field across the street from our friend Joe's house, when a strange figure appeared a few hundred yards away. "Is he holding a . . . *gun*?" I remember whispering nervously to Joe. *Pfffff!* I still remember the distinct whistling sound as what we thought were bullets sang through the fall leaves. The sniper's hooded form stood menacingly across a ditch on top of a hill in between two houses. In the moment, we had no idea that it was Joe's brother shooting at us or that he was using a pellet gun, not an actual rifle. We just knew we needed to run for our lives. I remember sprinting away as hard as we could, convinced that we were being hunted by an actual James Bond assassin.

We had been running from our unknown assailant for about twenty minutes when the situation heightened. Joe's brother ended up shooting him right in the forehead, the pellet lodging just below his hairline. I don't remember where I was when Joe went down, but I do recall getting separated from my friends and diving into a ditch Navy SEALs style. I then army crawled for a hundred yards before I buried myself in leaves. I hoped to be camouflaged long enough to take a breath before I sprinted to a neighbor's house to beg for help. That's when my friend Justin came lumbering down the suburban streets. "Miiiiike! It's Joe! He got shot! By his brother!"

The scene that met my eyeballs when I walked into their kitchen was like a movie. It was equal parts comedy and horror. Joe's brother had the pellet gun thrown over his shoulder, and he was standing over Joe's flailing body, wielding a butcher knife and screaming, "JUST LET ME CUT IT OUT, YOU CRYBABY!"

Joe wouldn't relent. "NO WAY! YOU SHOT ME! YOU SHOT ME! AND NOW YOU WANT TO CUT OPEN MY BRAIN! WAIT TILL MOM AND DAD FIND OUT ABOUT THIS!"

Until I stopped running, I didn't realize how much energy the adrenaline had sucked out of me. I collapsed into a chair and joined the growing rebuttal of this attempted, amateur surgical procedure. Joe was finally driven to the hospital, where an actual doctor removed the pellet and sent him home with three stitches. I think Joe's brother was sent home for the rest of his life once his parents found out he had been hunting his brother and friends like a serial killer.

IMAGE IS EVERYTHING

At the end of the day, the actual threat against our lives that day was perceived. I guess a pellet gun could kill you, but the odds of dying from a BB are probably less than dying from a slip and fall in a grocery store. The point is, a perceived threat still feels like an actual threat. This is definitely the case when it comes to an argument. It also means that I may not make a habit of creating enemies, but that doesn't mean other people won't make themselves into my adversaries. Threats tend to come for us when we begin to argue, don't they? Stand up for anything and you'll quickly find yourself in someone else's crosshairs. Maybe your initial reaction to the title of this chapter was rebuttal: *How can I live like I have no enemies when people insist on turning against me? What do I do when I'm trying to argue peacefully while people continue to threaten me?*

This is quite the question, particularly against the backdrop of the pandemic years. The last few years have felt like threat after threat, haven't they? I don't know about you, but I've felt hunted by both sides of every polarizing issue that has emerged from the news outlets. Let's agree that cultivating a compassionate middle isn't quite as click worthy as an incendiary headline. Living through a pandemic has forced me to contend with the idea that we often view one another not only as selfish but also as outright threats to our well-being. I thought that much of what people were arguing about were gray places, but I quickly found that many folks didn't share my perspective.

What particularly fascinated me was the correlation between feeling threatened and making threats. It seemed the people I found myself arguing most heatedly with were the ones who felt the most threatened. Whatever aspect of the pandemic felt scariest to someone seemed to determine when they threatened me and what they threatened me about. While some feared spreading a virus, others feared spreading misinformation. Some feared catching the virus while others feared having their freedoms taken away. We all got scared in different ways, and when we feel threatened, the gray can quickly turn black and white. Fear has a way of making enemies of us all. When the grace of the gray begins to fade, it's hard to remember that *people are not the enemy.*

Now, I don't deny there are times when we must defend against, incapacitate, and generally thwart some people from enacting harm on others. This is not a chapter about the complicated reality of the police or the military's role or pacifism, per se. Rather, I'm focusing on threatening discourse. These are usually the times we tend to perceive a greater threat than what is actually there. However, most of us aren't having the types of arguments on any given day where our lives are truly being threatened. It's usually just our egos that are at stake.

Consider a few scriptures with me here. First:

> God has shown me that I should not call anyone profane or unclean. (Acts 10:28, NRSV)

When arguments arise, are we quick to label certain people as "profane" or "unclean"? Before you breeze over this, let me ask you: Are Democrats unclean? Are Republicans? I'll speak a bit more to politics in a moment, but I have to admit that I've heard friends and family, depending on which side of the aisle they vote, utter certain politicians' names like a curse. We must refrain from calling groups of people unclean. I'm all for discussion and disagreement surrounding policies, but if we believe every person bears the image of God, we must refrain from demonizing any person who holds an opposing position than we do. Second Corinthians 5:16 adds, "From now on, therefore, we regard no one according to the flesh." God knows their hearts and why they vote the way they do; we don't. We almost always make assumptions based on what we can see. God reminds us to look deeper.

Here's one more verse:

> The god of this age has blinded the minds of unbelievers, so that they cannot see the light of the gospel that displays the glory of Christ, who is the image of God. (2 Corinthians 4:4, NIV)

Now, I recognize this says "unbelievers," but I think we could stretch it to cover anyone who doesn't see things the way we do. Paul says the minds of unbelievers are "blinded." My friend Tom says he visualizes people as blind prisoners of war who don't even know they're prisoners. This allows him to feel empathy where he previously felt fear. It allows him to have compassion where before he brought contention. I think this is a fantastic way to view the people we disagree with and those who scare us the most profoundly. Imagining those we fight with as hostages might help us move toward them in compassion rather than shudder in terror. It also helps me considerably when I remember how many times I've been proven wrong. That means I'm often the blinded hostage who doesn't know it. This is humbling. When it comes to conflict, image changes everything.

If someone is shooting real bullets at you, I'm not saying you ought to try to hug them. What I am saying is that we need to view people differently when we are in the throes of hot debate. Although we're not under the threat of physical harm, our rising pulses and adrenaline often blind us to the reality that we aren't actually in any real danger and that the people we disagree with aren't our real problem. Even though it feels like it, people are not the enemy.

I don't care if I have to repeat this until I'm blue in the face. People are not the enemy.

No, really.

People are not the enemy.

Here's why:

> We do not wrestle against flesh and blood, but against principalities, against powers, against the rulers of the darkness of this age, against spiritual hosts of wicked-ness in the heavenly places. (Ephesians 6:12, NKJV)

We do not wrestle against flesh and blood. I know that's a tough pill to swallow. When someone is screaming at you from the car next to you on the highway or giving you an all-caps rebut-tal on your Instagram page or holding you at box-cutter point, it sure feels like the problem is flesh and blood. But Paul insists that our real problem is fourth dimensional. He says we wrestle against principalities, powers, rulers, and "spiritual hosts . . . in the heavenly places." Maybe you are starting to squirm as you read this. Maybe you have some wounds or baggage around talks of the devil and his minions. I understand the reaction. I've been in rooms where well-meaning pastors make it sound like there's a demon hiding in every nook and cranny. I get it. We do plenty of harm when we blame everything on the devil, but we also do harm when we dismiss the realities of the unseen realm. It seems we can make mistakes on either side. We give the devil either too much credit or not enough. As the movie *The Usual Suspects* reinforces, "The greatest trick the devil ever pulled was convincing the world he did not exist."[1] If that was the greatest trick, then his second greatest was convincing the rest of us he's everywhere.

While some of us give dark forces too much credit, I would say most of us in the modern age go too far the other way. We don't shiver in terror at the thought of demons; instead, we buy movie tickets and make popcorn. We are often in danger of trivializing the demonic to the point of farce. We scoff at the idea that there is a real realm full of dark forces. This is just as problematic as over-obsession. Think on this for a moment. When we completely discount the unseen, we are left with only humans to contend with, and so people become the whole of the problem. When that happens, people must be the enemy. There isn't any other option. But when we consider "the heavenly places," it frees us to see the world and all who live in it differently. It's why the weapons of our warfare are things like praise, prayer, and forgiveness. When we have eyes to see that our enemies are spiritual, we will fight differently.

You might pause here. *Easy for you to say, Mike. You've never met my family. You've never met the people at my church. Please don't go blaming their wrongdoing on demons. You didn't hear the way they talked to me. I've heard this my whole life, and people end up using this passage to dismiss their own responsibility. They need to own up. They're the ones who hurt me, not some demon.*

You are spot on. Make no mistake. They do indeed need to own up to their participation in sin. I'm not discounting that at all. I don't think Paul means that every argument gone wrong is the devil's fault. But I do think he's urging us to consider that there's always more to the story than we think. This helps me particularly in the arena of disagreement. When someone says something acutely murderous, I'm able to stop and gain perspective before spewing venom back at them. It helps me pause. It helps me forgive those who hurt me when I consider that they are responsible but that they may also have some inner demons inherited from generations past.

FOLLOWING THE MODEL OF JESUS

I can't think of a better example of separating someone's actions from the evil forces behind them than Jesus's response to His crucifixion. Do you ever wonder what He was thinking on Calvary while the centurions were pounding nails through His flesh? He said, "Father, forgive them, for they don't know what they are doing" (Luke 23:34, NLT). I don't know about you, but I'm left shaking my head. How could He say the centurions didn't know what they were doing? They were the ones inflicting death on Him, after all. They were certainly participating in it. But, according to Jesus, other forces were at work as well. Although the centurions were the ones doing the physical harm, they weren't the ones Jesus saw Himself wrestling against. He saw another realm at play.

This blows my mind. It's paradigm-shifting to realize that Jesus looks past the action and sees the heart. I don't know about you, but I tend to think the exact opposite when I'm wronged. I think, *Oh yes, they do! They know exactly what they're doing.* But how incredibly arrogant of me to think that I know better than Jesus why someone is doing what they're doing.

So, if it wasn't the centurions, who was crucifying Jesus? Who was He fighting against while hanging on the cross? According to the apostle Paul, Jesus "disarmed the powers and authorities" and "made a public spectacle of them, triumphing over them by the cross" (Colossians 2:15, NIV). He disarmed whom? He wasn't disarming the centurions, obviously. They still had their spears and swords. When I read this passage, that's whom I think Jesus should be disarming. He should be humiliating those centurions for thinking they could get the best of the Son of God! But Jesus's life wasn't being *taken* from Him, was it? He was laying it down.

Jesus was fighting an unseen enemy. And He was fighting by dying. The powers and authorities, while using their might and their force, were being disarmed by Jesus's sacrifice. The powers and authorities, while trying to make a spectacle of Him, were instead made into the spectacle. They were seen for who and what they really were. They were exposed. How? Jesus disarmed the threat by succumbing to it. In doing so, He turned enemies of God into friends. It turns out shame's power is no match for love.

Jesus saw past the physical weapons and set His focus on taking away the spiritual ones. He let the centurions keep their armor and hammers. He let them keep their whips and crosses. He let them keep their taunts and accusations. But, ultimately, He took away the weapon of shame. In the unseen realm, He exposed the real enemies and He triumphed over them. At the cross, as Jesus was being murdered by human hands, He once and for all disarmed the devil. Jesus's triumph allows us to look deeper with Him. We begin to see the real problem.

Thanks to Jesus, we can learn to distinguish between the principalities and the person. The next time you're verbally attacked, try whispering to yourself, "Image of God," over and over until it sinks in. Or maybe, "Forgive them, for they don't know what they are doing." Regardless of who is standing in front of you, try whispering prayers of healing over them as a fellow image bearer instead of contending with them as an enemy. Remember, when it comes to enemies, *whom* you see as the real threat changes everything.

DISAPPOINTED BY JESUS

When I think of my own life, I'm certainly grateful Jesus sees past my worst behavior. I'm relieved that He sees all the forces at play. He labels me not by my mistakes but by His love.

This should come as no surprise. He also refused to label His followers by their pasts or even their political persuasions. It's amazing to see how politics never came between Him and His friends. Unlike in today's vitriolic climate, where we would see party lines, Jesus saw an opportunity for reconciliation. In particular, I'm perplexed by the radical friendship between Matthew the tax collector and Simon the Zealot. The Zealots were radical. They believed Israel should never be governed by anyone other than itself. They believed the Jewish people should be completely free and should take back the land the Lord had given them, by whatever means necessary. For Simon, Matthew would have been one of the vilest members of society. In the Zealots' eyes, a Jewish man getting into bed with Rome and collecting unjust taxes from his own people was the epitome of the word *traitor*. The Zealots would have killed people like Matthew.

Matthew, on the other hand, could have easily loathed someone like Simon. He may have thought of the Zealots as obtuse and unlearned. Matthew might not have even seen anything wrong with collecting taxes in the first place. He was just doing his civic duty, right? The government had been put in place by God, had it not? Someone had to collect the taxes, didn't they? Why not him? I can't say with certainty, but I imagine guys like Matthew would have thought, *Hey, I'm just doing my job.*

Why do I bring up these two apostles? What do they have to do with disagreement? Well, to think of them in modern terms, imagine the Zealots akin to something like the militant alt-right and Matthew as something like the CNN-spouting left. Viewing them merely by the externals, these two were bound to be enemies. Honestly, when I really consider just how opposite these two were, I'm left wondering, *How on earth did both of these men walk alongside Jesus for three years without killing each other?* And perhaps more importantly for us, *How do we learn to do the same?*

I really don't know how Matthew and Simon got along, but it must have had something to do with relearning who their enemies were. For them, following Jesus must have meant constant reframing. It also must have meant constant disappointment. I know that sounds strange, but as you read this, aren't you just a tad bit upset that I'm saying the person who hurt you or votes differently than you doesn't get to be your enemy anymore? In light of our built-in desire for justice, it sure stings to think of mercy being not only for us but for the ones who threaten us too.

Many of us forget what sort of ideas the disciples had around who Jesus was meant to be. All their presuppositions were perpetually being torn apart. Jesus didn't come as the political messiah they had envisioned. It's why they couldn't seem to understand what He meant by saying He was going to die. Jesus didn't overthrow the government like they had imagined. It's why Peter came running in with a sword drawn, making salami out of a Roman's ear. Jesus didn't give them the power they had expected. It's why James and John bickered about who'd sit on which throne. The disciples were anticipating a political and social revolution, not a spiritual one. Their enemies were in the tangible, physical here and now, not in the unseen realm. They were ready to crush their enemies under their feet, and Jesus was supposed to lead the charge. Isaiah even said of the Messiah that "the government shall be upon his shoulder" (Isaiah 9:6). But Jesus didn't lead the charge against physical forces; He came against the invisible ones. I wonder if we're not just as disappointed as they were.

If you were a disciple expecting to be a part of a military conquest over Rome, imagine how bewildered you would have been when Jesus tossed a coin around and said, "Render to Caesar the things that are Caesar's" (Luke 20:25). Imagine the mystified shock that would have spread across your face. I'm sure the disciples were absolutely crestfallen. Instead of coming to destroy Roman rule, Jesus came to subject Himself to its iron fist. Instead of preserving the temple, He said, "Destroy this temple, and in three days I will raise it up" (John 2:19). Instead of calling the disciples to eradicate God's enemies, He said, "Bless those who curse you. Pray for those who hurt you" (Luke 6:28, NLT). Instead of reinforcing their biases and prejudices, Jesus deconstructed them. Everyone must have been at least a little disappointed in Jesus because He wouldn't agree with them on who their enemies should be.

I think some Christians are similarly disappointed to hear that spiritual powers and authorities are the real enemies we are fighting. It's much more exciting to stand up to a bully than to pray for the one who's doing the tormenting. Marvel movies would be a lot less entertaining if Spider-Man just swung around and prayed for bad guys. Let me repeat, I'm not necessarily advocating for pacifism. Sometimes a bully needs to be disarmed. But I believe seeing past the bully helps us see when we need to create peace in certain situations. It undoubtedly allows us to tread more lightly in the gray spaces.

The chorus of the U2 song "Invisible" reinforces this point beautifully. Bono croons, "There is no them. There is no them. There's only us. There's only us."[2] Jesus is teaching us the same thing. We have to see past party lines like Simon and Matthew did.

We have to stop seeing the people we're afraid of as enemies to be struck down. How differently would we communicate with the ones who threaten us if we realized they weren't the real threat? What if we saw everyone we argued with as a blind prisoner of war who needs to be rescued? Of all the confusing, shocking things about Jesus, His unrelenting insistence to de-villainize His enemies strikes me the most profoundly. Keep in mind, Jesus even called Judas to come and follow Him. What's more astonishing is that Judas was seemingly more disappointed in Jesus than Jesus was with Judas.

LOVING JUDAS

The idea that Jesus continued loving Judas must have finally gotten through to the four gospel writers. Each one refers to Judas Iscariot as "one of the twelve." Matthew and Mark do this several times, in fact. Can't you see how revolutionary this is? I would think the wounds Judas inflicted were so great that the gospel writers wouldn't have any grace left for the likes of him. You'd think they would exclude him, but they didn't. They didn't oust him. He was still "one of the twelve" in their recollections. To Matthew and John, he was one of the twelve who walked with them, ministered with them, broke bread with them, and slept on the dirt with them. He was Judas. And yes, as the gospel of John reminds, he was "Judas, who betrayed him" (John 18:2). But I think it's worth our meditation that these writers still called him their own. Even in hindsight, you still see them saying, "He was one of us."

Has anyone let you down as profoundly as Judas did the disciples? How do you view them? What Judas did to Jesus and the disciples was way more intense than the things we tend to squabble about. After committing the deepest betrayal, Judas then took his own life. I'm heartbroken to think how many of us wouldn't want to associate with someone like that. I'm in awe of the disciples' posture. I am most undone by how they truly learned what it seems Jesus was trying to communicate to them all that time. People are not the enemy.

Jesus was always assimilating the wrong crowd, wasn't He? He was perpetually bringing in close the "wrong kinds of people." He hung around with the tax collectors and prostitutes; He drank from a well with an adulterous Samaritan woman. He kept eating in the houses of Pharisees. He always bore with the ones that others thought were unbearable. Whether they voted blue, red, socialist, or libertarian, whether tax collector or Zealot, a centurion or a betrayer, Jesus called all to His table. Sinner, saint, tempted, or weak—everyone had a seat.

With Simon and Matthew, Jesus showed He loved every person from every political party. With Judas, He showed He is with the ones who can't even love themselves. And with Peter, I think you could say He showed He is even rooting for the deconstructionists. Not everyone who deconstructs walks away, do they? Peter may have denied Jesus in the heat of the moment, but ultimately he had been given the keys to the kingdom. I can't help but wonder if Paul had Peter in mind when he wrote in his epistle, "If we are faithless, he remains faithful—for he cannot deny himself" (2 Timothy 2:13).

Judas and Peter were remarkably similar, weren't they? Imagine what would have happened if Judas, like Peter, could have hung on just a few more nights. By the sound of it, the other disciples seem to look back on Judas with an aching, wishing he, too, could have made it just a few more mornings like Peter did. Peter easily could have gone the same way in his denial and subsequent shame. If only Judas could have made it to that breakfast on the beach. Jesus asked Peter three times—once for every denial—"Do you love Me?" I can't help but wonder what would have happened had Judas made it there. Would Jesus have told him, "I love you" thirty times? Would He have asked, "Will you balance the checkbook again? Will you start with the silver you were paid? Would you believe you are worth more than that silver to Me?"

Where we see enemies, Jesus sees children and future children of God wrestling under the lies of fear and shame. He sees the demons on our backs. He calls to convict, not to crush. I'll speak a bit more about that later, but that makes sense, right? The disciples knew how much they all needed grace. All but John had scattered when the centurions came to the garden. It would stand to reason that they would extend the same grace to Judas that they had received themselves. I firmly believe Judas might have written his own epistle if he had only hung in there a few more nights. Never forget, on the night He was betrayed, Jesus washed Judas's feet.

A PRAYER FOR ALL OF US

If you're like me, you need to constantly remember that we are called to love everyone, even those who have wronged us, even those who have threatened us. When Jesus was being hammered to a cross, He turned to prayer. I imagine He might have been recalibrating amid that pain to remember that even those centurions were not the real enemy. "Forgive them, Father, for they know not what they do." If Jesus needed to pray in His most desperate moments, how much more should we? I invite you to practice praying a prayer like this one:

Father, remind me of Your love. You love every centurion swinging a hammer. You love every Judas and Peter, Matthew and Simon. You love every enemy I create and every enemy that comes looking for me. You love the sinners and You love the Pharisees. You love the prodigal sons and the older brothers. Awaken me, Holy Spirit. Open my eyes to see the real battle. We do not battle against flesh and blood—it's so hard to remember. Help me see. Help us see. Open my eyes afresh. Please protect us from making any person an enemy. Protect us from wrongful perception. May we see how you see. Jesus, teach us to lay down our lives for others. Redirect our anger. We pray against the schemes of the devil. May we resist the labels he would have us believe. May we be known for our love, not for our war-waging. In Christ's name we pray.
Amen.

5

Kissing the Fool

It will do you no harm to find yourself ridiculous.
Resign yourself to be the fool you are.

—T. S. Eliot, *The Cocktail Party*

If we approach disagreement believing that the source of the problem lies only with our opponent, we will never find a loving way through. Perhaps we'd do better addressing the enemy in ourselves first. I'd love to see more of us adopt the attitude of G. K. Chesterton, who once replied to a *Daily News* editor, "The answer to the question 'What is Wrong?' is, or should be, 'I am wrong.'"[1] In other words, before you see someone else as a threat, maybe take a moment to recognize that the threat might actually be you. I'm chuckling to myself as I write this because I've found the only way to even begin to converse with someone you oppose is to first recognize how many times you've already opposed yourself.

What do I mean by that? Well, think back through your life. If you go back just fifteen years, chances are you'll think to yourself, *Man, I was an idiot back then.* So, follow my logic here. If, by your own estimation, you were an idiot fifteen years ago, chances are fifteen years in the future you'll look back and think, *Man, I was an idiot.* Which means you are currently an idiot—and by your own account! I know from experience.

And I would add this: Owning up to your own foolishness is key to dealing gently with others in the gray spaces. None of us is perfect. We need only consider our own stories to be reminded of that. And it should go without saying that we all do foolish things, even if it takes us years to finally own up to them.

We are fools, and we need help.

Quit fighting it.

Go ahead and own it.

Or as I prefer to say, "Kiss the fool." (That's a bit gentler and carries more fondness than saying "Own your ignorance.") We can't expect to be gentle with the fools around us until we learn to be kind to the fool staring back at us in the mirror. Kissing the fool means accepting the fact that you're dumber than you currently think you are. Kissing the fool means opening yourself up to outside information. Believe me when I tell you, disagreement will start to sound like wisdom when you learn to kiss the fool. Once you accept it, you can stop playing the fool. You might even begin to become wise.

I told you I know from experience. I couldn't kiss the fool, and I paid dearly for it. Sure, I ended up getting kissed in the process, but let me tell you, kissing myself would have been so much better. The kiss I got turned out to be the single most embarrassing moment I've experienced in my life so far. I stress *so far.*

HIGH SCHOOL FOOL

When I was in tenth grade, I didn't want to kiss the fool in the mirror; I wanted to kiss a senior named Madison. I had a gargantuan crush on her. In the name of disclosure, her name wasn't really Madison, but I'm calling her that to avoid any further embarrassment in case she reads this one day. Though I was two years younger than Madison, I was absolutely positive she returned my fancies. No one could tell me anything different.

I was a fool, and I was delusional.

All my friends told me so. They told me to accept my Madisonless future and see what a fool I was. I couldn't do it because, in my mind, I had irrefutable evidence that our nuptials were an inevitable reality. You see, we had already kissed once the year before, so my suspicions weren't exactly ill founded. Okay, saying "we kissed" might be a bit of an overreach. Make no mistake, I definitely kissed her. Actually, it was more like a lip tag, and I might have tricked her into it, so some might think it didn't really count in the first place. But to me, it counted. Oh yes. It counted.

It was after a cast party following the finale of the spring school play. This was the end of my freshman year, and I had already been crushing on her for the previous six months. I saw an opening and I took it. As the last of the stage props were stowed away in storage bins, I brazenly marched up to her and said, "Hey, Madison, I bet you a dollar I can kiss you without using my lips." She cast me a dubious squint. My bombast had successfully surprised her into a brief bout of illogical paralysis. Pure curiosity taking hold of her imagination, she conceded. "Okay, then," she whispered passionately. (Thinking back, maybe it wasn't "passionately.") Without further warning, I pecked her like a city pigeon snatching food crumbs off a sidewalk. She stumbled backward in surprise and yelled, "HEY, YOU USED YOUR LIPS!"

I swaggered. "Well, I guess I lost my dollar."

I hesitate to tell this story because I don't want to give any other misguided youth any ideas. Had she not had a sense of humor, she could have had me arrested. I hope as you hear the conclusion of this story, it will thoroughly dissuade you from repeating my stupid little stunt.

You see, Madison and I didn't talk to each other about that moment for the whole next school year, but I knew she remembered it and was desperately pining for our next lip session. I boasted to my friends every chance I got. I told them about my romantic moment and how I had obviously cast an irresistible spell on an upperclassman. My friends tried to talk me down from my ledge of certainty, but I wasn't having it. "If you walk a tightrope with a net, you're asking to fall," I would say. "Besides, if she wasn't so entirely super into me, why did she kiss me back?"

"She didn't kiss you back," they contended. "She just couldn't get out of the way fast enough."

The way she avoided me in the halls, I knew she was playing hard to get. She wanted me to chase after her. I knew it was only a matter of time until we made our relationship official. (Did I mention I was delusional?) Again, no one agreed with me. Everyone tried to talk some sense into me. It was pointless. I knew the future, and it was full of Madison.

Then it happened—the moment I had been braggingly anticipating for twelve months. Madison asked me to come outside.

We were at my friend's house, at a group party watching some home video of something that I don't even remember. Everything around "the incident" is kind of blurry. But the next few moments with Madison are crystal clear. They're etched into my memory, chiseled in stone. She didn't have to ask me twice to come outside. I ran after her like a puppy for a treat. I was really more like a convict marching punch-drunk to the gallows. I just didn't know it yet.

As soon as we had cleared the front walkway of our friend's front yard, she spun to face me and grabbed my hands. "Dance with me!" she crooned into the night. "Dance and sing to me!"

She didn't have to ask twice. I quickly obliged. Fiercely muttering gratitude to heaven, I swooped her up in my arms and began to dance with all my sixteen-year-old might. I thanked the Lord for all the times growing up that my mother had made me dance with her in the kitchen. I had the skills. I was ready. I was made for this moment.

We came to a stop in the street. I stared into her eyes with what I thought was a mesmerizing gaze. To her, I probably looked like a homicidal maniac. My eyes bulged and my smile began to twitch. I was coming undone. We hadn't done anything more than exchange pleasantries in the hallway since my stunt the year before. You can imagine my surprise when she looked at me and said, "Recite that soliloquy you performed in theater class. You know, the one from *Romeo and Juliet.*"

Did I know the one from *Romeo and Juliet?* Are you kidding me? It was all falling into place. She was crumbling under my wooing! I was Romeo! She was Juliet. We were those star-crossed lovers and Shakespeare's words were never fully realized until this magic moment. I took a breath to calm the rattlesnake heart suddenly thrashing wildly against the cage of my chest. "Why, yes," I stammered. "I know that one."

I closed my eyes in concentration, recalling the hundreds of rehearsals I had performed to my pillow throughout the previous months, and repeated those lines she was begging to hear. The effect on her was clearly instantaneous. "Come over here," she said as she tugged on my now-noodling arms that were losing their strength at her caress.

She whispered, "Let's stay out here for a while. Let's look at the stars."

I bit my tongue to hide an involuntary squeal of delight. I stifled the response I wanted to blurt: *No need to look up! I'm already staring at a supernova.* But I reined it in. Instead, I simply croaked, "Ye-ar-ah-ha." Somehow, she understood my noise to mean yes, and before I could process what was happening, she was again pulling me by the hand until we were lying side by side on the hood and windshield of her car.

I was entirely triumphant. *I knew this was coming!* Again, I had been bragging about it for over a year to anyone who would listen. I told friends. I told strangers. I told the guy bagging our groceries at the local supermarket. I talked so much romantic smack about Madison, I knew this was simply the unavoidable conclusion of asserting my destiny into the universe. There was no other alternative. I had spoken my truth, and I was being rewarded. I named it, and now I was claiming it. Eat your heart out, Tony Robbins.

Steeling my nerves, I took the wheel. I jumped from the car and beckoned for her to join me. I danced with her once more, but this time I was leading. I locked eyes with her and noticed . . . *Was that hesitation?* I shook off the notion. I spun her once, twice, and finally a third time, ending in a low dip. I pulled her up with a bit too much bravado, because she stumbled into me, landing with her hands on my shoulders. She glanced over her shoulder at the driveway of the house. *Was that confusion on her face?* I gently touched her chin until our eyes met once more. This was the time to make my move. I had waited long enough. It was time to pronounce our mutual love. What better way to seal the moment than with a kiss?

This time it was going to be a real kiss. It would be a kiss that far surpassed all other kisses. Cue *The Princess Bride*.

Madison glanced around furtively as I leaned in. As my face closed in on hers, she pushed back ever so slightly against my chest. I stalled for a second, but then the moment of surrender arrived, and she gave in. Our lips met. Oceans roared. Asteroids collided. In holy reverence, the universe stopped expanding. The world stopped spinning. The angels in heaven rejoiced. I didn't move. I didn't breathe. I dared not let even one hair on my head shiver. I stood there frozen, nothing but my lips quivering uncontrollably. I did not want to disturb the serenity of this eternal moment.

After something like three seconds that felt more like three lifetimes, Madison pulled away. She blinked. I thought she was trying to return from the ecstatic oblivion that I was still floating in. She wasn't. She was just trying to wait for the perfect moment to finally say, "Umm, April Fools'?"

Suddenly, the sliding door on the van in the driveway groaned open and ten of our friends tumbled out into the grass. Bellowing laughter burst from the open doorway and echoed off every molecule in the night sky. The earth began spinning again, only this time it was hurrying to catch up. My world went from slow motion to fast-forward. My eyes shot feverishly back and forth between my friends (if you could call them that) and Madison. My hands went cold. My stomach dropped into my feet. Galaxies imploded all over the cosmos. My used-to-be friends began to high-five, and Madison mouthed a silent "Sorry" in my direction before firing at the dogpile of spectators now howling in the grass, "You guys were supposed to come out before he kissed me!"

They didn't hear her, but I did. I was scuttling back toward the house, doubled over from the pain of embarrassment. I found a table in a corner and threw myself under it. My stomach was a black hole. My entire being was being sucked into a weightless abyss. I huddled in the dark and waited for the waves of nausea to subside.

The words of Proverbs 3:7 boiled in my brain. "Be not wise in your own eyes." Then I heard Proverbs 16:18 come right on its heels: "Pride goes before destruction, and a haughty spirit before a fall." *DANG IT, BIBLE!* I screamed in my head. *I don't need an "I told you so" right now!* It was too late. I grew up in Christian school. There were plenty more where that came from. Proverbs 11:2 finished me off: "When pride comes, then comes disgrace, but with the humble is wisdom." *Figures Solomon wrote those,* I thought as I attempted to nurse my aching ego. *He had his own lady troubles.*

Needless to say, things didn't work out between Madison and me. But twenty-five years later, I'm glad that incident happened. They say tragedy plus time equals comedy. I've indeed learned to laugh at myself thanks to this moment. Not only did I still get to kiss a senior (April Fools' still counts), but I also learned to kiss my own fool. I learned an invaluable lesson about certainty and the way that wisdom works. I learned I needed to listen to counsel. I was so dead set on a determined end that I couldn't hear the cacophony of voices pleading for me to listen to reason. I learned to be a bit more careful about what I assert. In fact, my friends were probably so tired of coming up against my resistance, they decided to turn my own assertions against me. I refused to embrace my foolishness, and it returned to me tenfold.

Solomon, and whoever else may or may not have written the book of Proverbs, knew this well. It's why the book of wisdom goes on and on about how wisdom works. "In an abundance of counselors there is safety" (11:14), and "in abundance of counselors there is victory" (24:6). "The way of a fool is right in his own eyes, but a wise man listens to advice" (12:15). "A fool gives full vent to his spirit, but a wise man quietly holds it back" (29:11). "Do not rebuke mockers or they will hate you; rebuke the wise and they will love you" (9:8, NIV).

That last one gets me to this day. The wise will love you for pointing out their blind spots. I can't think of a more convicting thought. Do I love to be told I'm wrong? Do you? If I could learn to love to be shown where I'm wrong, I might just save myself a whole heap of embarrassment. Lord knows I could have saved myself a van full of friends laughing hysterically at my blinding thickheadedness.

Here's the question for us moving forward: Where are your Madisons? It's a tough question, and it probably doesn't do you any good to ask yourself. If you're like me, you're going to need some outside information. You'll need some help seeing your blind spots. We all do. But what if we could just accept the fact that we all play the fool sometimes? What if we weren't afraid to embrace our own ridiculousness? What if that really is the way to wisdom?

For me, I'm learning to ask where my Madisons are. I'm kissing the fool in the mirror by learning to admit that I constantly need intervention. I'm learning to see there's more gray in me than I previously thought. And you know what? The sooner I kiss the fool that I've been, the more readily I have compassion for those I consider fools now. We really do all play the fool sometimes. We've all dug in our heels along the lines of black and white, only to find our footing was all wrong. Don't be afraid to be disagreed with. In fifteen years or so, who knows? Your position could turn out to be false, no matter how certain it feels right now. You might just end up disagreeing with yourself down the road, so be open to others' dissent in the here and now. If I had learned that lesson a little sooner, I could have saved myself a mountain of embarrassment. But you know what? Madison did let me kiss her, so maybe I wasn't the only fool in the equation.

The Smug Monster

I have yet to find any support in the Bible for an attitude of smugness: *Ah, they deserve their punishment; watch them squirm.*

—Philip Yancey, *I Was Just Wondering*

"Resign yourself to be the fool you are," advises T. S. Eliot.[1] I would add, "Don't just resign yourself but embrace yourself." Put your hands on the cheeks of the fool looking back at you in the mirror and give them a big fat kiss. You are a fool, and it's okay. Believe it. Embrace it. Trust me on this, because if you resist it, you'll eventually be played for one like I was. Or worse yet, you'll assume everyone else is a fool. And *worse* worse yet, when that happens, you will wind up a fool who is completely alone.

How do I know that? Because Proverbs 14:7 implores us, "Leave the presence of a fool, for there you do not meet words of knowledge." That's great advice, unless we never admit we can be foolish too. Think this through. If you can't ever own your occasional foolishness, you'll be left to assume that *everyone else* is the fool. And according to this verse, when you find yourself in an argument with a fool, you will need to leave. So, if we find ourselves constantly thinking everyone else is the fool, then we'll quickly find that we will never be able to have a conversation with anyone.

To put it plainly, when we refuse to hear critique in any form, it shuts down discourse. When that happens, we become caged in our own echo chambers, and as a result, the ensuing isolation is of our own making. It distorts the way we see. It distorts the way we discourse. It eventually turns us into something a little less than human. I have a term for this kind of degeneration. I call it the *smug monster*.

What is a smug monster, you ask? I don't think I have to answer that, because chances are you're already thinking of somebody who is one—which paradoxically might also mean *you* are one. But essentially, to me, a smug monster is a creature that used to be human but, for one reason or another, could never—under any circumstances whatsoever—admit they were wrong. I guess you could call it the "I am always right" monster, but that just doesn't have the same ring to it, does it? Remember, our objective in this book is to learn how we can lovingly disagree. Well, there's no way forward with someone who won't ever listen to the other side. I'm sure you've experienced this. A smug monster excels in shutting down conversation before it can even begin.

Now, it's easy enough to spot a smug monster in someone else. Just look for the condescending smile, the folded arms, and the impenetrable platitudes that keep every argument and counterpoint at bay. A smug monster thrives on that hardening in the spirit that cements one's rightness into immovable fact. However, identifying this trait in ourselves is easier said than done.

Merriam-Webster defines *smug* as "highly self-satisfied."[2] Think about that. Self-satisfied means you're right and you know it. Some synonyms for *smug* from the same source are *assured, biggety, bigheaded, complacent, pompous, vain.* The word *biggety* made me laugh, but smug monsters probably wouldn't find that funny because they are rarely ready to laugh at themselves. Smug monsters are all around us and, more concernedly, always looking for the smallest footing to start growing in us. The more you find yourself thinking of all the people you know harboring a smug monster–like spirit, the more likely it is that you're the one *they're* thinking of having that same spirit.

Everyone knows a smug monster, but no one thinks they are one. Self-satisfied means you see only through your own eyes. This means that for us to sense our own smugness, we will often need outside help. Imagine if every day a new layer of film grew on your eyes. The world would get darker and darker, but because you got used to each new layer, you wouldn't notice the darkening or loss of clarity unless someone else pointed it out to you. That's a scary thought. The only way to keep a check on whether you're turning smug is to ask the people around you.

YOUNG SMUGS

When you're going smug, the last thing you want to do is ask anyone anything. My sixth-grade daughter is a prime example. She has got plenty of smug to spare. She knows everything. No, seriously—she's twelve years old, and she thinks she knows *everything.* Absolutely everything. I suppose it's equal parts beautiful and terrifying. The unflappable certainty she wields is complete and immovable. She knows math. She'll tell you so. She figured it out. Don't even bother her with a proof. Science? Oh, she crushes science. Math, science, Wall Street, Dow-Jones index, principal interest on loans, and how the federal government is falsely suppressing inflation. She knows it all.

I'll ask her, "Hey, do you want me to show you how to mow the yard?"

She shrugs me off. "Oh, no, I totally know how to do that."

"Do you need me to help you with your reading assignment?"

She scoffs. "Dad, this is so easy."

"Want me to explain your homework?"

"Father, I've already graduated med school."

"Oh," I counter. I had no idea my daughter was Doogie Howser.

Now, either we are amazing parents for instilling such a grandiose self-confidence in her, or we have set her up for looming disaster. What will happen to this blessed child of ours when her overconfidence finally meets up with her actual lack of understanding? I should tell you she is quite bright, and that is also the problem. I suppose it's the blessing and the curse of being born on the intelligent side. If you're naturally bright in some areas, it's easier to be unaware of how dim you are in others. Admittedly, she comes by her overconfidence honestly. The smug apple doesn't fall far from the tree.

You see, I have had plenty of personal struggles with smugness. When I was young, I had a teacher in high school give me a stark evaluation after a summer theater program. He said that while I was generally charming and deft at making friends, I was terrible at truly learning the content he was teaching. He said I wasn't interested enough. Now, I could argue he wasn't a very good teacher, but I think that would only compound the point. A young smug's only interest is showing off what they know, not in exposing what they don't. When you're young, or at least, when I was young, there's this nagging need to compensate. It's truly a scary thing to admit how much you have yet to learn. Especially when you haven't come to the realization that you're so deeply loved despite it all. There's a big old crazy world out there, and to assess yourself accurately feels pretty overwhelming, doesn't it?

I, for one, was desperately trying to construct some form of ego, trying to find some footing and identity. All these years later, I still have trouble with it. But the more I'm aware of how deeply known I am by God, the easier it is to be honest about what I don't know. It's also what I'm trying to teach my daughter—to be known by God frees us up to admit we don't know what we're doing, because we rest in the fact He does.

I imagine Paul was acutely aware of the young-smug tendency when he was addressing the church of Corinth. At the beginning of 1 Corinthians 8, he explains how "'knowledge' puffs up, but love builds up" (verse 1). He goes on to say that "if anyone imagines that he knows something, he does not yet know as he ought to know. But if anyone loves God, he is known by God" (verses 2–3). I love how Paul sees and calls out this strange correlation between knowing and being known. If you imagine you know everything, you aren't known. How strange of a sentence is that? It's profoundly strange and wondrously true. Vulnerability sets us up to encounter the love of God. It's worth noting that Paul seems to put quite a bit more stock in loving God than thinking you know something. Perhaps he knew that when you love and trust God, you don't need to play the game of appearing wiser than you are.

I have to say, I wish I believed that earlier in my life. My daughter is slowly coming to this realization. No one enjoys talking with a know-it-all. A shining barrier of superiority becomes a blockade around our hearts. When you don't need anyone else's wisdom, it's hard to remember how much you need their love.

Maybe the two are meant to go hand in hand. My daughter doesn't need to impress God, and consequently, she doesn't need to impress others. But she sure does need intimacy with both. I pray she doesn't have to go through the kinds of humiliation I had to endure to really arrive at this truth.

Looking back, I regularly thank God for striking down the smug monster that was incubating in my heart that fateful April Fools' Day. With astonishing force and accuracy, a single joke removed my blinders and kept me out of a prison of my own making. But as it turns out, young smugs are quite resilient. The young smug in us can lie dormant for years, only to grow back with merciless speed given the right environment. I guess you could say smugness is like kudzu. It's an invasive species. Left unattended, it will come back tenfold even after being hacked and trimmed. The pride of a smug spirit must effectually be pulled out by the roots. Otherwise, it limps along, waiting for a time to grow again. I'm sad to admit it, but being embarrassed wasn't quite enough to kill mine off for good. My smugness found its chance to flourish again a few years later when I went to work for a church.

I'M SO AWESOME

A couple of years into college, my band became the house band for a local high school ministry. After that, I was asked to lead music for the college ministry. Then I was made the director of worship for the young adult ministry. Finally, I was given the reins to the student-led worship service on campus at my university. With each promotion, my seeming prominence and power grew. I didn't yet know that power was for service. Underneath the surface, lurking and feeding on all the visibility and notoriety, my smug monster tendencies were growing like a baby in the womb, nourishing on the praise.

Let me just say, that didn't have to be the case. I hope you see that. The positions I was given didn't need to make me unteachable. But that's the worrisome thing about smug monsters. The more power they receive, the more they must pursue ways to intentionally subvert that power. Otherwise, smugness pounces on prominence like Homer Simpson on an all-you-can-eat donut buffet. The good news is, holding this spirit in check is the simplest thing in the world once you lay your ego down. Of course, simplicity doesn't make it easy. Defeating the smug monster only ever requires the one simplest but hardest thing: letting the light in.

Give those around you the freedom to tell you how it is, and watch the smugness shrink back in horror. This is really all it takes. However, it's not a one-and-done sort of treatment. As basic as it is, this act of welcoming instruction must be constant and consistent. It's like mowing your yard. If you keep up with it, it's a pretty easy task. But if you let it grow for a month, it will take all afternoon to cut down the weeds. I didn't stay on top of the smug monster within me because I didn't know how it worked. I didn't know it was waiting for a chance to overtake me, so I did the worst thing you can do. I stopped listening altogether. I stopped asking for criticism in any form.

Again.

This time, it wasn't romance blinding me. It was my newfound prestige. Regrettably, I not only gloried in my fame, but I also thought being a leader meant acting like you knew everything. I thought being like Jesus only meant you try to be more perfect. And so, I thought asking for help was a sign of weakness. The more I saw myself as the be-all and end-all, the more my promotions felt like stamps of approval instead of new reasons to invite alternative perspectives. I didn't see my position as a chance to serve; I saw it as my chance to be served. The beast inside was beginning to roar again. I began thinking of myself as "the guy." The more I believed the hype, the less grace I had for anyone who might disagree with me. I became less humble and far less teachable. I stopped asking for help. I stopped inviting others in. People became rungs on the ladder I was climbing. I started stepping on them instead of seeing them. It turns out that smug monsters are both deaf and color-blind. They don't appreciate the gray at all.

My wife recalls meeting me around this time. We wouldn't start dating for another three years, and now I know why. She has even dry-heaved talking about how I would act back then. She says she couldn't get close to me because I reeked too badly of arrogance. I guess you can also tell when someone's turning smug by the aroma they leave. With that being the case, I was deaf, color-blind, and I stunk. I had no idea, though, because I was the local "worship guy." How could I be guilty of anything? I was fixing folks left and right. I had all the answers. I would counsel everyone I met, even when they didn't ask for it. I had spiritual platitudes ready for any situation. I can even recall sitting down a seventy-year-old deacon in the church to give him some advice that he certainly wasn't asking to receive. My wife says I would throw out Bible verses at people like a prescription-happy doctor in bed with a pharmaceutical company. I was never the patient, mind you. I was the solution. Yikes. I was the definition of a smug monster.

Let me pause here, before I share yet another ridiculously humiliating moment, to turn our gaze to Jesus. We must never stop marveling at how the Son of God took on flesh. It's one of the most basic assertions of the Christian faith but dizzyingly profound. For God to become more human to save humans is stunning to say the least. If there was anyone who never needed advice, it was Jesus. And yet, He subjected Himself to our experience. He didn't pull us up; He came down. He didn't save from on high; He descended into hell. I've mused that Jesus didn't fix our brokenness until He felt it for thirty years first. He feels it before He fixes it. Why?

Because Jesus shows us that the road to salvation is a path of becoming more human, not less. Follow me here. Jesus didn't have to wait all those years to save us. What's the point in living among us for so long without doing any actual saving? What's the point in sharing our weaknesses, our burdens, and our temptations? Theologians have offered endless volumes of wisdom on this solitary point, but in this context, I think it's worth considering that Jesus did not only suffer for us but rather with us. He saved us by becoming one of us—which might mean that our duty on the path of following Him is to resist the smugness that strokes our egos. What do I mean by that? I mean the Pharisees were the religious party of Jesus's day. They learned massive amounts of information about God. And yet, instead of softening them, their knowledge made their hearts harder, more rigid. Jesus shows us that true holiness is marked by increasing love and tenderness. Perhaps that tenderness doesn't come from the lists of information that we can prove we know but instead from a deep knowledge of who we understand we are known by.

I know that at times in my life, I certainly had no interest in growing in compassion. I would never have seen the value in becoming more human. I couldn't be bothered with feeling anyone's burden; rather, I just wanted the glory in "fixing them." I've since learned a valuable lesson, thanks to my wife: Sometimes she doesn't want me to "fix it." She just wants to know I feel it. I now know the health of our relationship is built on knowing her heart, not her to-do list. And I'm sure this is true of situations outside my marriage.

While working at a megachurch, I was fixing everything and feeling nothing. Ironically, even though I was surrounded daily by humans, I was becoming less of one. I was busy dousing others in my opinions, and I was growing more and more uncoachable, un-teachable, and uninterested in any moment when I was the one learning. I was like Eustace in Lewis's *The Voyage of the Dawn Treader*. I was interested only in being the one to hand down wisdom from on high, and in doing so I was becoming a bit of a dragon. *Oof.* It hurts to think about. I was like Moses striking the rock, but all the while my pride was the thing that needed striking. Turns out, like Aslan peeling back Eustace's dragon scales, God was good enough to strike down the monster I was becoming. And He used the last person I expected.

BRENNAN MANNING THROWS DOWN THE DRAGON

Oh, the freedom that humiliation brings! I really do pray that God doesn't have to humiliate you to teach you, but it sure seems to be the way He likes to do it. This time, my embarrassment came at the hands of one of my favorite authors and communica-tors. My band was asked to lead music for a spiritual emphasis week at our college. I had just graduated and was obviously the correct choice for the conference. *Who else has put in the hours of practice and knows the pulse of the people?* That's what the now fully formed monster-mind was whispering to me, anyway. The school announced, to much fanfare, that my band would be leading the music. I reveled in it.

Later that week, after the school announced Brennan Manning would be the speaker for the conference, I knew beyond a shadow of a doubt God was putting me on the fast track to global spiritual domination. (Domination? *Ahem.* I meant influence. Or did I?) To say Brennan Manning was a hero of mine would have been a gross understatement. After reading *The Ragamuffin Gospel* in my freshman year of college, I had made it a point to read every other book Manning had ever written. I committed several of his paragraphs and anecdotes to memory.

In the several days leading up to the event, I found myself practicing some breathing exercises, just to keep myself from geeking out. I was elated. With me leading music and Manning speaking, this conference was undoubtedly going to bring order to the galaxy.

But here's the thing: I had no real interest in God changing the world. I certainly had no interest in letting Him change my world. That's for sure. My only real interest was in being the one through whom God would do His changing. This was a dire distortion I was painfully unaware of at the time: I didn't want the Savior to do His thing; I wanted to be the one doing the saving. Manning was about to expose that distinction.

The first two nights of the conference went off without a hitch. The cosmos was bowing under our skill and sanctity. God displayed stunning power and might through the words that were spoken but especially through the music. Yes, the music was undoubtedly the best part, if I do say so myself (and I definitely did). Before the third and final night, the leadership team gathered to pray over the last session. I smirked as everyone took turns praying wildly long-winded and overly articulate prayers. *Posers,* my monster brain croaked. It seemed everyone was more intent on proving their spiritual prowess to Manning than in submitting themselves to God. Why couldn't they be as great at being a Christian as I was? *I don't need to impress anyone,* I mused. *I know I'm awesome.* Manning wrapped up the prayer time by sitting in silence for a few minutes. He then muttered one of the simplest prayers I'd ever heard a speaker utter. It was something like "Abba, thank You for loving us. We are Your kids. We love You too. Amen."

I was still pondering the exactness and raw candor of his words when the unthinkable happened. "Thank you, Brennan," breathed the director of student activities. "Now, is there anything we can do better to improve this last service?" Manning sat up, swiveled slowly in his chair, and looked directly into my eyes. "You, young man?"

"Yes." I bristled and sat up straighter. It was the first time he had addressed me publicly and directly.

"Last night you did a terrible job. I left my message on such a tender moment, and your band got up and played a very raucous set. It was completely inappropriate. The next time, you ought to listen to the Spirit."

Inside, my chest howled and thrashed madly, wounded in a fit of rage. I wondered if the room could hear the cage bars rattling. It took everything I had to keep my face from contorting hideously. I glanced around the room. I cleared my throat. "I'm sorry, Brennan . . . What was that?" My ears were actually ringing with embarrassment. My "always has to be right" behemoth had never been punched so squarely in the face before.

"Listen to the Spirit next time," Manning reinforced.

He swiveled back and closed out the meeting with a few last words. I heard none of them. I was still clutching at my chest and sweating from the vertigo I was experiencing. It was, perhaps, the first time anyone had ever criticized my worship tactics. It was all falsehood and flattery up to that point. It was definitely the first time I had the ears to hear the criticism, anyway. Maybe they weren't all praising my methods like I thought they were. That's the funny thing about smugness. Once the spell is broken, and usually by someone you admire, it quickly unlocks a memory vault full of what everyone else has been trying to say. Just like my friends warning me about my Madison delusion, I immediately began thinking of all the much-needed criticism others had been trying to give me all along. It would seem humility is ready to receive wisdom from anywhere, no matter the source. The lightning bolt of realization when Madison said "April Fools'" happened again when Manning squarely put me in my place.

Want to know the worst part of what Brennan Manning told me? He was absolutely right.

For hours I thought of every possible retort. *He's just old*, I thought. I tried to dismiss his perspective. *He doesn't understand college kids. He's a speaker, not a musician. What does he know, anyway?* The rebuttals came fast and furious until I finally caved and welcomed the blow. And like a spell being broken, the moment I did, my ego shattered and my heart came back to life. This is the only way to strike down the smug monster. Over and over, we must desperately open our ears to hear what others are trying to tell us. Unlike Brennan's, their opinions won't always be right on, but our spirit to receive criticism can be. At every turn, we must open ourselves to critique in hopes that we don't let our scales grow back and harden against what could be wisdom.

When it comes to argument, what if we readied the arrows of engagement to hit the bull's-eye squarely on our own chests first? What if most of our agitation and anger and disagreement is really just our smug monster squirming? What if much of the hostility we feel is really just pride spilling over from our unchecked egos? If we're going to learn to have grace in the gray spaces, our own unnecessary black-and-white lines must be dealt with first.

I understand it's a lifelong process. We must allow ourselves to be disagreed with if we ever hope to gain the trust to lovingly disagree with anyone else. But I sure hope it doesn't take you the same abject humiliation to get to this understanding as it did for me. The good news I want to offer you is that Jesus can indeed show us the way. If the wounds from a friend can be trusted, how much more should we trust the scalpel in the hands of the Great Surgeon? The more we come to Him, the more we just might see that every time He disagrees with us, it's for our good. And perhaps we will grow to find the good in others' disagreements as well. What's even better news is that this all begins with a simple shift in our spirit. Before we even begin to listen to the voices outside, we will start with correcting the voice in our own heads. Our egos will tell us that there is nothing to be gained in leaning in and listening well. When that happens, all it takes is learning to whisper the four magic words to watch the spell of smugness break.

7

The Four Magic Words

If one has the answers to all the questions—that is the proof that God is not with him. It means that he is a false prophet using religion for himself. The great leaders of the people of God, like Moses, have always left room for doubt. You must leave room for the Lord, not for our certainties; we must be humble.

—Pope Francis, in a 2013 interview

When the smug monster rears its ugly head, we must learn to speak back. If we are ever going to create a safe space to hear the truth about ourselves, it's imperative we have the right words to speak against the clawing ache inside our chests. We must remember a new humanness is always waiting for us on the other side of the simplest four magic words: "I could be wrong."

I know. Those probably weren't the words you were expecting. Me neither. But believe me, these four simple words are magic. They really are. They can undo an incredible amount of arrogance and shame every time they're uttered. They are utterly succinct, but when uttered, they open expanses. They unlock doors. These four words can build bridges where there was previously no way over. They can hack pathways where there was no way through. They shift our perspective when all we could see is our own way. I'm telling you, try whispering them to yourself right now, and watch the change affect everyone around you. After all, if we're ever going to find grace for one another in the gray, we will have to acknowledge that there is gray to be had in the first place, won't we?

Go ahead. Try it out. Say it out loud even if you're in a crowded room reading this.

"I could be wrong."

Say it again.

And while you're at it, try adding the words "and that's okay."

I know. People might stop and stare.

Do it again.

"I could be wrong, and that's okay."

In case you didn't know, if the gospel is even the slightest bit true, then that means you are loved in your rightness and in your wrongness. We are all loved regardless.

So, we can say it again, and keep saying it, time after time: "I could be wrong."

I WANT A CHURCH THAT LOOKS LIKE TWELVE STEPS

My best friend is a psychotherapist, and he says healing always starts with the radical ownership of one's own faults. "I could be wrong" is the first tenet of Alcoholics Anonymous. It's actually a bit more intense than that. In AA, you must own up to the idea that you have mismanaged your life. Not only do they say "I *could be* wrong," but they add, "I *have been* wrong." Ouch. I know it hurts, but it's a necessary pain to make new paths through the gray. I believe this is such an important spiritual truth that I recently wrote this line in a song. The second verse of my song "All Together" says, "I want a church that looks like twelve steps where all are honest and accepted, but it's gonna take myself to cultivate the kind of life that others haven't seen yet."

It's kind of crazy, but I've learned that when it comes to arguments, each party is often waiting for the other to say these words first. When one side slightly cracks and says, "I could be wrong," movement toward one another can commence. If we embrace this first tenet of AA—that we not only could be wrong but have been wrong—we begin to have a lot more mercy for everyone. When that happens, we can begin to see the whole world in light of our own need of grace, not theirs. If I need grace, then who am I to withhold it from someone else?

When the world is wagging a finger at anyone who disagrees, I'm able to wag the finger at myself. Why? Because I have been wrong. Which is different than moping around saying, "I am wrong." See the difference? I'm able to own up to my actions without letting my actions become my identity. How? Because I don't need to save myself anymore. I have a Savior, right? I don't need to defend myself anymore either. I have a Defender. To me, anyone who claims to be a follower of Jesus ought to be one of the least defensive people on the planet. They, especially, can stand up straight while owning their wrongness, because even when they're wrong, they know they're still loved. They can say, "I *was* wrong, but I *am* loved." Just as the promise of resurrection causes death to lose its sting, when you know you're loved, arguments lose their venom. A Christian should be able to stand up and exclaim most freely, "I could be wrong!"

I CAN'T BE WRONG

A few years back, one exchange with a well-meaning youth pastor really cemented this observation for me. I didn't mean to cause an uproar. Between mouthfuls of reheated spaghetti, I just sort of half mentioned a hypothesis: "Yeah, I've been reading an interesting book that has a unique perspective about the creation story in Genesis 1."

"What is *that*?"

I looked up from my soggy pasta and met the eyes of the hungry young youth pastor sitting a table over. I didn't know he had been listening.

"Oh." I laid my spork down and straightened. I could tell by the look in his eye that this was going to be interesting. I continued, "I just read this book last week called *The Lost World of Genesis One*. In it, the author suggests the Hebrew words for 'Let there be' are better translated 'Let them have this purpose.' So maybe the creation story isn't an answer for where matter comes from, but rather it's answering the question 'What purpose does it have in God's creation?' If that's the case, then incredibly, Genesis 1 neither supports nor negates evolution or creationism. Pretty fascinating read; you should give it a go."

"I most certainly will *not* give such nonsense a go!"

His eyes bulged a bit grotesquely, and only then did I notice his full suit and tightened collar. I thought his head might actually pop off the top of his neck. *He's quite a bit more dressed up than the average youth pastor,* I thought.

He continued, "The text is abundantly clear that each day is an *exact* twenty-four-hour period of time! There is *no* other way to interpret that passage!"

"Huh," I mumbled as I returned to my dinner. "Well, I suppose it's not for everyone."

"You're *right*. It's not for everyone. It's for *wolves in sheep's clothing*. That's who it's for!"

He was staring into my eyes with the intensity of a thousand suns. I could tell I had hit a nerve. "Hey, man, I'm not sure why this is escalating so suddenly, but I hope you hear my heart. I've met too many kids who have been kicked out of their churches for believing in evolution. I hate to see that. Rejecting evolution doesn't seem essential to following Jesus, as far as I can tell. In fact, there are a lot of commentators who ponder the poetic nature of Genesis and what it's really seeking to convey. I'm just interested in keeping the main things the main things, you know?"

I'll spare you the details of the rest of the conversation. Let's just say it definitely escalated. I'll also add that I'm recounting this story because it was one of the few early times I miraculously kept it pretty cool. As I've said before, I haven't always seen the beauty in holding my tongue while holding the tension of an exegetical debate.

But I hope you hear what I've sadly found true in many faith circles: The acknowledgment of any form of doubt or any other possible interpretation, to some, is inadmissible. This would explain why some churches aren't known for their welcoming spirit. It might also explain the myriad of denominations in the American Protestant church alone. Maybe it explains why so many kids I connect with through my platform are scared to talk about their biggest questions with anyone in their faith community. And maybe you're shaking your head as you read this. Maybe you're ready to put this book down because you suddenly feel that by welcoming room for doubt, I'm trying to lead people astray. But maybe we'd find a deeper grace and unity if we stopped putting so much importance on nonessentials.

It seems to me, one of the biggest reasons we lose grace in the gray is that we turn certain areas that could be gray into black-and-white issues. Particularly for many, when it comes to matters of faith, to acknowledge any form of inquisition is to set your course for shipwreck. I've watched friends struggle with their beliefs online, only to be met with open hostility instead of gracious discourse. I'll write more on this in another chapter. But for many, merely questioning a previously held interpretation of Scripture feels dreadfully equivalent to questioning the inspiration of it altogether. I hope you can see those two things aren't quite the same. Sadly, when no one in a church can give any room for any uncertainty in themselves, visitors pick up on that energy. When we aren't gracious with our own questions, how are we ever going to create atmospheres of invitation for those who don't currently think or believe like we do?

I guess it could be stated that, to me, it seems some churches simply aren't concerned with inviting anyone new to the table. Trust me, I've been to a few of those. But for many others, I think admitting a little chink in the armor of our beliefs might just be the thing that causes those who are deeply struggling to say, "Maybe I belong here after all." I just want to hear my pastor say on Sunday morning, "I could be wrong." They don't need to say it all the time. I'm not even saying the pastor should believe they are wrong. But if a pastor would say, "I could be wrong," from time to time, I really believe it could change the game for many.

Without that opening, how do we truly keep a heart of invitation? If, as it says in Revelation 22:17, "the Spirit and the Bride say, 'Come,'" then the prevailing hermeneutic of the church ought to be inclusivity: *Bring your heart. Bring your mistakes. Bring your perspective.* If pastors are to err on either the side of exclusion or inclusion, I think they ought to err on the side of inclusion.

I used to believe the opposite. I used to think I wanted a pastor who was certain about everything. It made me feel good that even though I had questions and doubts, at least they didn't. But now I see I was using their faith like a Band-Aid, just covering the surface. I didn't want to really deal with my questions because I didn't want to learn to trust God; I just wanted to be right about Him. Certainty is easier than trust, after all. It took me a long time to realize that. Even if I knew all the "right things" about God, it wouldn't do me any good unless those beliefs led me to actively putting my trust in Him. This all might seem a bit dense, but even though cultivating healthy discussion around dissenting interpretations of certain benchmark scriptures is a dizzying task, I believe it's a necessary one.

Let me pause here and acknowledge that I'm talking about my experience in the American evangelical church. I want to note that in many faith traditions, inquisitive exploration is not only allowed but also encouraged. For instance, Judaism canonized the Torah (the Written Law), but it also venerates the Talmud (the Oral Law). The Talmud is filled with arguments between rabbis grappling with the meaning of certain texts. This means that the arguments themselves, in some respects, are considered sacred. This is a radical idea for many of us Westerners. When it comes to God, we're brought up to believe that the meaning of our sacred texts is always clear. This is, unfortunately, for lack of better words, obtuse. If you do any bit of work and read through just a few commentaries, you'll quickly find that's rarely the case. Begin learning ancient Hebrew or Greek or Latin and you'll find words that have no English equivalent. The more I read through opinions on certain texts by men and women who've given their whole lives to understand them, the more I'm left breathlessly whispering to myself, "I could be wrong."

For some people, the mention of an alternative idea is as unsettling as taking out the last piece of a teetering Jenga game. Ultimately, though, did any of the church fathers say belief in the commonly held interpretation of the creation story was necessary for salvation? When it comes to debates of faith, we must constantly consider what nonessential beliefs we have subconsciously made essential. How else will we do this work without a more loving posture of disagreement? Sometimes I wonder whether correct interpretation is always the most important thing to God in the first place. What if the wrestling itself is what God is truly after? He did bless Jacob, after all, and renamed him Israel, which means "wrestles with God." Again, if the Pharisees are any indicator, it's possible to have the entirety of Scripture committed to memory and miss the point entirely. Here's a thought to consider: Could it be that merely reading a scroll and adhering to the principles can be done far away but that the one who wrestles with God must be drawn close?

THE WISDOM OF DOUBT

It's strange. The older I get, the more Ecclesiastes begins to make sense to me. Have you experienced this? I feel a camaraderie with the writer of that book I didn't feel as a younger man. It's like, "Oh, you don't have all the answers either? Oh man, now I feel like I can breathe in your presence."

As a college student, I remember reading the book of Ecclesiastes and thinking, *Wow, I'm shocked these words are considered sacred.*

Sounds a bit too questioning for my liking. If I'm completely honest, I didn't like the book because I didn't like the way Ecclesiastes made me feel. It seemed to have too many questions and not enough answers. I was young and a smug, after all. I didn't see the value in admitting I could be wrong. But as I've aged, I've found such comfort in the words there. To me, a quick read through that book seems to suggest that true wisdom includes at least a trace of acknowledged doubt. Or as singer Leonard Cohen wrote, "There is a crack, a crack in everything. That's how the light gets in."[1] If Cohen is right, then true wisdom is being able to assert your most deeply held beliefs and end them with the simple words that express the wisdom of doubt: "I could be wrong."

Again, I know you might think this feels a bit heretical. We like to think that all Jesus cares about is whether or not we believe all the right things about Him. This explains why our debates are so angry. When eternity is on the line, things tend to escalate quickly, don't they? But don't forget, Jesus squared off with the Pharisees and said, "You search the Scriptures because you think that in them you have eternal life; and it is they that bear witness about me, yet you refuse to come to me that you may have life" (John 5:39–40). This must mean Jesus is after something more than simply spouting off correct interpretation. He gave us the Scriptures so that they would ultimately lead us to encounter Him. Make no mistake, I'm not saying the Scriptures don't matter. They most certainly do. But if you've really encountered God Himself, you don't just talk differently. You hold things differently. You encounter others differently. Your posture changes. Maybe like Jacob, you walk differently. You walk with a limp of humility. Maybe like Solomon, you have your own doubt-laced thoughts, like the wisdom in Ecclesiastes.

This carries over from faith into everyday life as well. Whatever you believe about any topic or subject, if you can't preface your point of view with the four magic words "I could be wrong," rest assured, you will not invite relationship from anyone who thinks differently than you. The smug resistance of "I am never wrong" is like an electric fence keeping others out. There have to be cracks for someone to see you're a human, just like them. It's hard to have a relationship with a suit of armor. Sure, you might feel safe tucked away in there, but you won't feel close. Remember, to be in relationship, there must be room to disagree. Without that small crack in the door, there's no room to let anyone in.

I've often wondered whether the entire book of Ecclesiastes was included in the canon of Scripture simply to remind Christians that true wisdom still has this element of doubt or *humble curiosity*. Sure, the end of the book says, "The end of the matter; all has been heard. Fear God and keep his commandments, for this is the whole duty of man" (12:13). But it also says things like this over and over: "In much wisdom is much vexation, and he who increases knowledge increases sorrow" (1:18) and "'What happens to the fool will happen to me also. Why then have I been so very wise?' And I said in my heart that this also is vanity" (2:15). Disrupting questions like these are scattered throughout the book. I'm left to wonder, *Maybe these questions are a gift from God to remind us that even the greatest wisdom begins with the admittance "I could be wrong."*

DON'T SHOOT THE MESSENGER

A wild exercise you could try sometime is to flip through your Bible and every time you see the word *believe,* add the word *trust* beside or above it. Wouldn't you agree that God cares less about whether you believe you're meant to forgive someone and much more about whether you will? To say it another way, don't you think God would rather have His kids trust-falling into His arms than keeping their distance while acing their theology exams? I believe it's at the heart of what Jesus said about the Pharisees when He said they looked good on the outside but inside they were "full of dead men's bones" (Matthew 23:27, NKJV).

For more on this thought, I recommend Peter Enns's book *The Sin of Certainty*. To be honest, in the past I have hesitated to include any names of any authors or any books. Do you know why? It's been my experience that any time I quote anyone, there will be some who rise up and exclaim that the author has divergent beliefs in some areas, and consequently, I'm immediately scolded that I'm leading people astray. It's one of the most frustrating things I've encountered in my years of sharing from stages and on the internet. This only proves my point. Many people screen the source of the statement more than the statement itself because they don't believe others are able to search for the truth themselves. It's the epitome of throwing the baby out with the bathwater. We can't ever admit we're wrong, so the people we read or quote aren't allowed to ever be wrong either. We think always being right is more important than always being love. Or like Enns points out in his book, we think being certain about our beliefs is more important than letting our beliefs lead us to lovingly trust in God.

Because we can't ever admit we're wrong, we end up shooting the messengers. Don't believe me? Try this out sometime. Instead of *Where's Waldo?* I guess I could call it "Where's the Heretic?" Quote C. S. Lewis on your blog or social media but attribute it to Richard Rohr. See what happens. Then try the inverse. Quote Rohr but say it's Lewis. Henri Nouwen, Thomas Merton, Eugene Peterson—the list goes on. Or maybe attribute a Bible verse to Marilyn Manson just to really confuse people. Okay, maybe don't do that. But whatever you do, don't quote anyone who strays from what you believe specifically, and definitely don't quote anyone from other faith perspectives! At least, that's the message I've received. The problem is, it's not even consistent with the apostle Paul's evangelism tactics. In his sermon on Mars Hill, Paul quoted plenty of the modern philosophers of his day. How can Paul do that? I believe it's because Paul wasn't scared who said something, because he knew all truth was God's truth. To some that is not the way it is. We tend to separate who speaks what we believe and who doesn't, instead of listening to everyone and taking it to Jesus. To some, certain teachers are spiritual heroes who should be venerated; to other groups within the church, those are the people who must be properly labeled "dangerous."

This is a delicate issue, for sure. It is possible to be led astray. I'm not denying that. But what are we led astray by? Is it by our intellect or by our hearts? I admit, some have no problems with extrapolation. They can read all kinds of content and separate the meat from the fat for themselves. But others have a hard time doing so. My point is that as we grow in wisdom, I hope our nets would grow larger, not smaller, as we look to find God's truth in the world. We can begin to avoid automatically accepting or disqualifying information based on the source. Put simply, we must learn to separate what is truth from who spoke it.

I wonder whether we don't believe God when He says, "You will seek me and find me, when you seek me with all your heart" (Jeremiah 29:13). How many times have you recommended a book and felt like you had to add, "I mean, I don't agree with everything it says in there, but . . ."? As if there were a book you could read and say, "Yeah! I agree with the author 100 percent." If that is true, I'd like to humbly ask whether you're a follower of Jesus or a clone of a commentator. Isn't it just as dangerous to blindly trust everything someone says as it is to read someone you don't always agree with? It's also strange to me that certain authors like Lewis get a hall pass for saying some fringy things sometimes. Lewis, after all, dabbled in all kinds of ideas; he just framed those ideas in the context of works of fiction.

When I stop shooting the messengers, it gives me a healthy bit of distrust for all messengers. I don't discount something because of the source, and I don't automatically trust it either. Trusting someone's opinion unequivocally is just as unhealthy as distrusting them without exception.

It's worth adding that the religious establishment was constantly angry with Jesus because He was too inclusive. You might rebut that statement by thinking of Matthew 7:13 when Jesus says, "Enter by the narrow gate." But you must also remember the Jewish elite wanted to get rid of Jesus because He kept including Gentiles in God's plan for redemption. Jesus did say the road that leads to life is narrow, but it seems that He was saying the size of one's ego is what causes the squeeze. Remember the camel and the eye of the needle imagery. I don't think He really meant rich people can't get saved. Also consider this is the same Jesus who invited a thief on a cross into paradise. He's also the one who said the workers who were added in the eleventh hour were paid the same as the workers who slaved away in the fields all day. Jesus's generosity, not His rigidity, is what paved His path to Calvary.

I know I will probably be misunderstood here, so I'll try to explain. Having toured so much for twenty years and having conversed with so many believers from different factions of Christendom, I've found that the list of essentials—the beliefs that constitute Christian faith—is astonishingly short. Also, believe it or not, I've found that more of us agree on the essentials, the truly important things, than we would expect.

If you don't believe me, stop and think. Are things like alcohol consumption, political persuasion, or mode of baptism *essential* truths to be agreed on? I have plenty of friends who would say, "You better believe it!" They would even change churches over such matters. But when you take a step back, I think you'll agree that many of our denominations have been created over non-essentials. My sister spent five years in China, and she said one of the confoundingly beautiful things about the church there was that the lack of options really forced the people to drill down to the essentials. She said the list of essentials was a whole lot shorter in the churches there than it is in the churches of America.

I'll come back to what I think is essential and what isn't, but for now, I want you to stop and think. Are there places in your life where you haven't left room for the wisdom of doubt? Is there any room in your faith for mystery? Jesus said the size of the faith He requires is that of a mustard seed. He must mean that the size of your faith isn't as important as the quality of your faith. That is to say, the amount of faith you have isn't nearly as important as whom your faith is in. When you're resting in the ever-widening embrace of Jesus, you can be more brutally honest with yourself and with others. You might find yourself whispering in the comfort of His embrace, "I could be wrong, and that's okay."

8

Holding the Tension

Paradox has been defined as "Truth standing on her head to attract attention."

—G. K. Chesterton, *The Paradoxes of Mr. Pond*

Life is full of the tension between two truths, and that tension often disguises itself as paradox. Here are a few paradoxes to consider:

I discipline my children by giving them grace.

God displays His sovereignty by giving us free choice.

I serve others better by prioritizing taking care of myself.

The first shall be last.

I work from rest.

Four o'clock in the morning is so late, it's early.

On and on they go. Life seems to be teeming with paradox. If we can't admit that we can be wrong sometimes, the complexities of life will pull at our rigidity until we crack. If you can't muster up the courage to admit you could be wrong, paradox will pull at your strings until your arguments unravel.

We can either deny it, rage at it, or learn to accept it. Opening our minds to the tension can be quite painful, but I believe that if we learn to embrace it, we might just find ourselves becoming more gracious—not only with ourselves but also with everyone we meet. The difficulty with tension is that it demands we stretch. Jesus said to love with heart, soul, and strength, which to me means we must learn to stretch our minds and our hearts in the same way we must stretch our bodies. I suppose you could say grace makes us flexible. If we resist, our inflexibility will eventually snap under the pressure of life's unceasing tension.

ENJOY THE STRETCH

I've never liked stretching. I do it because I like to run and I don't like pulling a hamstring. I do it because I understand it's necessary to fight off decrepitude. But why must stretching be so stinking uncomfortable? I know . . . if it hurts, I'm probably doing it wrong. But even when I'm doing it right, it doesn't feel good. Sitting there motionless while all that static energy sends waves of discomfort shimmering through my muscles' nerve endings is not my favorite. I even do yoga sometimes, but begrudgingly so. Let's just say I've never been able to gently toss my legs over my shoulders like a floppy backpack. I'm just not very flexible.

Mental stretching is even more uncomfortable than physical stretching. Being stretched in my viewpoints may lead me to a healthier understanding of my own belief structures if I let it, but that doesn't mean I have to like it. To put it succinctly, I don't have to like holding the tension, but to find grace in the gray, I have to learn how.

The summer before I was in eighth grade, I was forced into a situation that demanded I stretch beyond what I thought humanly possible. My family took a vacation to Myrtle Beach. It was a sparkling adventure to that pearl of the Atlantic. Mini golf and dinner theaters as far as the eye could see. Beachwear shops strategically situated every quarter mile, boasting the very latest in fabric spray-paint art. It was all a middle school boy could hope for. I body-surfed the brown-green waters of the Atlantic from dawn till dusk. I proudly bore purple streaks of Zinka sunscreen, striped across my face like an ancient Celtic warrior's face paint. In between bodysurfing sets, I would sprawl across the sand and spend my recovery time making eyes at the girls on the beach. They were likely my age, or at least I hoped they were. They were looking at me too. Or were they looking at the surfer behind me? No, they were definitely looking at me. During the day, I was a thirteen-year-old beach king, brining in my saline glory. At night, I would stand mesmerized before the mirror, my browning skin perfectly complementing my oversized dress shirts. I would ogle my most recent acquisition from the Structure store at the local mall. I was trendy and trending in the right direction. I was, as the kids say, *feelin' myself.*

But all good things must come to an end, and as my week of sunbathed revelry was coasting to completion, my freedom suddenly came to a jarring halt with one simple, understated directive from my father. "Just climb in the back seat there," my dad said between exasperated breaths. The poor guy was busy stuffing our sedan while I was lost in my own head, reminiscing about all the almost-romantic encounters I had experienced that week. Even if they were all in my head and from several hundred yards away.

"What, Dad?"

His curtness yanked me from my stupor. "Back seat. Now."

Much to my horror, our family had taken in quite the souvenir haul during our week's stay in South Carolina. "But, Dad, there's nowhere to sit," I challenged.

My sisters and brother were already all sprawled out in our friend's minivan, laughing and reclining like Pharaoh's cats. I was the only child left needing a seat, and apparently my parents thought I could double as a human Tetris piece. My dad's near-ancient BMW was packed floor to ceiling, leaving one cubbyhole of space in the back seat next to the door.

"Sure, sure, there is, Mikey." He tried to sound cheerful, obviously spent from the physical and mental puzzle challenge he had been solving for the past hour. He was trying to stay upbeat, but he had come to the end of himself. "Here, just move those towels aside, and if you could pull your knees to your chest . . . Now just pull them a little tighter toward your chin. Hold your breath for a second. Push that pole aside so it's not in your rib cage. I think I can slide this watercooler. *There!*" he exclaimed as he snapped the door shut after deftly stuffing me in.

I sat among the spoils as we began cruising down the interstate. Sand-caked beach chairs and coolers heaped on deflated saltwater-soaked rafts jostled gently against loose pieces of luggage bursting at the seams with local commemorative T-shirts hanging from their not-quite-zipped sides. It was all pushing against my head and my nether regions and cramming me against the backseat window. I began to hyperventilate. Rumbling down the highway, all our vacation paraphernalia began swimming around, beneath, above, and beside me. I became one with the collateral. That's all I was in that moment: collateral damage. There were only so many seats, so I suppose someone had to take the torture. Someone had to become the sacrifice. Like Isaac on the altar, I played the hero quite well, if I do say so myself. All things considered, I held it together. Barely. It would have been an excellent mental exercise for Special Forces training. For six hours I sat there, knees to my chest, trying not to lose my sanity.

When we finally made a dinner and gas stop at the travel center Burger King, my door mercifully opened, and I breathed oxygen for what felt like the first time in years. Consequently, I and a myriad of our family's belongings poured out all over the parking lot. I slithered away from the car and onto the asphalt, only to find that I couldn't stand. Both my legs, from my hips down to my toes, were dead asleep. My family cackled as they jumped from the van beside us. I struggled to place my feet beneath me and began careening toward the restaurant. I toppled over three times before the blood came tingling like fiery icicles back into my appendages. I screamed in torturous delight as I regained feeling in my lower half, enough to finally stand erect and resemble more of a human than an amoeba.

"Come on. It wasn't that bad, was it?" my sisters barked jovially around me.

"Not that bad?" I questioned. "Well, whoever wants to trade spots with me for the last two hours is more than welcome." No one took the offer. It seems they didn't like holding the tension either.

I understand this is a ridiculous example. You might be mumbling to yourself, *Come on, Mike. Get to the point.* This is a book about gracious disagreement, after all, not child endangerment. But the point is simply this: Holding the tension must be learned. Holding the tension takes time. When you find yourself constantly blurting out your own opinion time after time, it might do you good to call this little story to mind. Simply holding in your opinion can feel like being caged in the back of a family car. It hurts, but the more we do it, the longer we can hold our position while hearing out someone else's.

Sure, some people have an easier time than others. In high school, I knew a girl who was a contortionist. She was oddly flexible from birth. But for the rest of us, stretching must be practiced. I am still notoriously bad at it. I couldn't do it in the back seat of my family's car, and after several failed yoga class attempts, I'm obviously still working on it. The practice of stretching our egos is even more demanding. When conflict begins, we must practice holding the tension. The art of compassionate listening begins with our ability to control our own breathing. When we learn to quiet our minds and take a moment to breathe, we might just find that we can begin to quiet down our own rebuttals. After that, we begin to make space to actually listen to the other person with every fiber of our being, instead of waiting for our moment to release our perspective. When that happens, we give each other the greatest gift. To listen is to be vulnerable. It is the gift we give when we allow the stretch. It is where we're able to share space where we couldn't before. Unnatural but undoubtedly necessary as it is, we want to get through the stretch as soon as humanly possible. Most of us don't want to sit in the back seat of an argument for one second longer than we have to.

My own aversion to holding a stretch shows up most poignantly in my marriage. When conflict arises, as it must in any healthy relationship, I want to shut it down immediately or resolve it. My wife, on the other hand, can live in the tension of a conflict for weeks or even months on end. She meticulously goes through what she's feeling as it simmers and stews. She percolates. She considers every angle. I should add that her ability to process helps her considerably. She gains perspective and clarity on her position as she examines every angle. She holds the tension by sitting in it.

Sometimes I'm in such a hurry that it feels like she's reclining in it. It could just be a matter of introversion and extroversion. I joke that maybe it's because she's had four children. She knows what it is to be stretched—figuratively and physically.

My wife can hold the tension. As a matter of fact, I think she loves it. She'll wait till a moment before I close my eyes to sleep to bring things up. Remember, I want to go to sleep in a peaceful embrace, gazing into her eyes while we drift off into euphoric prophetic visions from the Lord. But my wife will climb into bed and casually mutter, "Oh, by the way, I had some feelings tonight about what you said, but I don't really want to talk about it right now." Then she'll roll over and ask me to turn out the light.

Now, it is excruciatingly mature and marvelous of her to be able to hold the tension so comfortably, and it's utterly agonizing for me. I lie there aghast, thinking, *I thought we weren't supposed to let the sun go down on our anger! Aren't we supposed to resolve everything before we let ourselves sleep?* But I've come to realize, she isn't doing what I think she's doing. She isn't avoiding conflict; she's holding the tension. She isn't accidentally letting something slip out before she goes to bed. She's telling me at that precise moment because she wants me to know there's something wrong, and she also isn't allowing it to stew and boil into something uglier by not addressing it.

Of course, as a very inflexible tension holder, I lie there next to her, unable to sleep or dream for hours. I don't want to address it unless there is a definitive resolution right then and there. I should note that not letting the sun set on your anger is not the same thing as coming to a place of tranquil, harmonious synergy. The gray space of tension makes my brain buzz. I think through every single thing that I could have possibly said or not said. I try to call to mind subconscious childhood trauma. I think of every wrong motive I have ever had in my entire life. I begin to wonder whether she can see into the secret desires of my soul that are unknown even to myself. I wonder whether she's writing divorce papers in her dreams. By the time the alarm clock sounds the next morning, my wife wakes up to find me puffy faced, red eyed, and fitful. I'm full of every possible kind of dread that can bewitch the human psyche. Meanwhile, she just smiles and says, "Did you sleep all right?"

"Did I sleep all right?" I bellow. "Did I sleep all right? OF COURSE I DIDN'T SLEEP ALL RIGHT! I did not sleep at all because you hate me and everything I say!" Like I said, I need resolution.

Lately I've been reading articles that suggest couples can promote health by creating a fight schedule. I think it's probably a good idea for any relationship. It's why companies have reviews, isn't it? This ought to be common sense. When you're living in close quarters with anyone, it's a good idea to write down the grievances and conflicts that pile up between you. Don't write things down to blast the other person; write them down so you know what needs to be worked on. Set a date on the calendar where you know you'll get the chance to air out the laundry.

The idea here isn't to keep tabs on your spouse's or roommate's wrongdoings. Keeping track of what needs to be addressed is the heart of it. Having a finish line or a date to look forward to can help you hold the stretch a bit longer instead of just holding it as long as you can. It's why I stretch my calves for thirty seconds at a time. The measurement gives me a goal. Setting a fight schedule also gives you a time to talk through your differing points of view when they aren't so emotionally charged.

Do something similar with your loved ones. Having a time and place to work through a disagreement is essential to taking much of the emotional charge out of things. Just like we don't want to discipline our kids when we're angry, we ought not to debate from that heart space either. Disagreeing in a spirit of love is the goal, right? Working through conflict at a later time can help clear the rage that fogs our brain waves in the moment. It's like stretching after you're warmed up a bit.

But the questions remain: *How do I actually do that? How do I hold the tension with my wife, my kids, my friends? How do I hold my tongue when it feels like I have to speak?* What's more, *How do I hold the tension in all my relationships? How much tension should I allow to exist in my beliefs about God or in my conflicts with strangers on the internet? How far do I let my listening legitimize an opinion I wholeheartedly disagree with? How much tension can I keep before my muscles snap back in protest?* I've worked to address some of these questions in the subsequent chapters, but for now, I want you to try to take an objective step outside the culture you grew up in.

EASTERN/WESTERN

I grew up in a Western mode of thinking. For those of you who did as well, I want you to know it isn't right or wrong, but it indelibly informs the way we see the world and ultimately how we learn to disagree. We in the Western Hemisphere are historically less pre-pared to hold tension. I would even be so bold as to say we are dramatically underequipped in this area. We aren't often seeking a compassionate middle ground; we want to divide the world into winners and losers. The Greek systems that helped shape our sys-tems of thought taught us a very certain way of seeing things.

Western thought is more absolute.

Eastern thought is substantially less binary.

In other words, I grew up either-or.

I'm learning to swim in the mystery of both-and.

A quick look into Eastern-inspired viewpoints reveals that our Greek-trained ways of thinking don't always have solutions for the questions that arise. There tends to be more mystery than we had previously envisioned.

Ray Vander Laan was the first teacher to really blow my brain open in this area. It just so happens that he studied under a myriad of rabbis in Israel for years. When I was in college, a friend downloaded a few MP3s of his lectures on my iPod, and they really helped me realize how limited my viewpoint of God was. Later, I watched some of his seminars online and was transfixed for days as he opened my mind to an entire realm I hadn't considered before. I felt like Peter Parker, mouth agape at Doctor Strange opening the multiverse in front of me. Vander Laan was my Doctor Strange of the Bible. (Ray doesn't wear a cape or anything. He's quite unassuming, in fact. I met him once at the Michigan high school where he's taught for decades.)

For instance, in one of his lectures, Ray asked a classroom of students something to the effect of, "What does God smell like?" The classroom sat in dead silence. He said, "Well, any good Hebrew scholar would tell you, 'Burnt meat and incense.'"

He followed it up with, "What does God taste like?" Another long pause ensued. "Honey! Because the psalm says, 'Your word is like honey on my lips.' A rabbi will show up in a kindergarten class with a honey bear in hand. He'll dab a drop of honey on pieces of wax paper and remind the five-year-olds, 'Don't forget! That's what God tastes like!'"

You see what I mean. I had never before heard anyone ask, "What does God smell like?" Ray continued to blow my mind with his teachings on the dust of the rabbi. He widened my perspective on Psalm 23 when he explained that "green pastures" were tufts of vegetation spread through the desert outside Jerusalem where the shepherds would lead their sheep in the cool of the morning. The promise of lying down in green pastures wasn't sheep wearing sunglasses and drinking martinis. It was a promise that my shepherd God would lead me through the wilderness of life while providing just enough provision for each new day. Ray continued to challenge me with prompts like "God is _____ (fill in the blank)." I think, *God is love. God is peace. God is all-powerful.* He would counter with images: "God is a fortress. God is a shield. God is eagle's wings." He would say that a Western-educated mind uses abstract words while thinking about concrete ideas. An Eastern-educated mind uses concrete images to wade in the waters of abstract ideas.

I had a lot of tension to consider.

The BibleProject has become another resource that has left me quite fascinated by the limited lens through which I interpret paradoxical realities. The Shema is recorded in Deuteronomy, and part of it reads, "Love the LORD your God with all your heart and with all your soul and with all your might" (6:5). The word *nephesh* in Hebrew appears more than 750 times throughout the Scriptures, and the word is unfortunately translated into English most often as the word *soul*.[1] In a BibleProject teaching, Tim Mackie and Jon Collins argue that in the Hebrew Old Testament, it is more commonly translated as the word *life* and that its most basic meaning is "throat." It is meant to convey the "essential physicality of a person."[2] In other words, a person doesn't have a nephesh; they are a nephesh. But the BibleProject teaching takes it a step further. It says your soul is the total composition of everything that makes you who you are. Your body and mind and heart are all included in what makes up your soul. This means that what you do with your body affects your heart and that what you do with your mind affects your body.[3] It's all connected, and it's why Proverbs says things like "Envy rots the bones" (14:30, NIV). It all adds up. You are the sum of all your parts. I am not simply a body and a soul like my Greek way of thinking had led me to believe. I am so much more complicated than that. And so are you.

WHAT'S THE POINT?

In this chapter I have jumped from sitting in a cramped car to having arguments with my wife to unpacking the Western versus Eastern mindsets that we bring to our interpretations of Scripture. I rounded it all up with the Hebrew word *nephesh*. Now that I remind you of that, you're probably thinking, *How are these all related?* Remember what I said at the beginning of this chapter? We must stretch. We must stretch our entire nephesh. We must allow ourselves to be made flexible in our bodies, our minds, and our hearts. I want you to see that tension is actually everywhere we look. I want you to see that in order to give others the gift of gracious disagreement, it might require holding some real tension on your part. I'll hear friends say they can't believe in the Bible because it contradicts itself. I would argue it's exactly why I've come to trust it. The Scriptures read a lot like life. Like the book of Ecclesiastes with its wisdom of doubt, I trust these texts because they aren't scared to show me how paradox seems to fill the universe. It's in our relationships; it's in our reasoning; it's buried down in our very souls.

Physically.
Emotionally.
Spiritually.

The tension between truths is everywhere we look, and if we can learn to embrace it, holding the tension will help us grow.

We hold the tension until we stretch.

We hold the tension until our lives are full of flexible grace.

We hold the tension until we can hold our opinions while hearing another.

We hold the tension so we can hold the ones we love.

And maybe we can begin to reframe how we experience disagreement in every aspect of our lives.

Arguing with Children

The great enemy of communication, we find, is the illusion of it.

—William H. Whyte

I'm a songwriter. I've been a bandmate. I'm a husband. Each role has given me the . . . umm . . . *opportunity* to face disagreement. Playing in a thousand churches, writing a thousand songs, and working day in and day out in the mysterious realm of music has given me more experience in discord than I'd ever imagined possible. And, yes, I've maneuvered my way through a thousand interpersonal band fights over the years too. And, yes, my wife and I have also learned that finding a way to stay in love requires we not only call a ceasefire but also learn to appreciate each other's differences.

But perhaps the aspect of my life that has given me the most hands-on experience with traversing disagreement has been my role as a father. Not everyone has this particular experience in common, nor is it necessary for learning the elegance of gracious disagreement. However, for me, most of what I've learned about navigating nuance has been from learning how to father my four daughters.

Yes, I have four daughters. Your prayers are appreciated. Having four daughters is great. It just means someone's always crying in my house, and sometimes my girls cry too. Tears are everywhere and incessant. I can't tell you how many times I've had to admit that I could be wrong, hold the tension, deal with my smug monster, and kiss my own foolishness while parenting these daughters of mine. Little girls will love you affectionately and blast you unapologetically in the same breath. I have had to learn to grow several layers of thick skin while keeping an ever-softening heart. It's no easy task. Now, if you've ever found yourself in the room with four sisters, you might have an idea of why I find this important to tell you. Siblings can torch one another like no one else. If you haven't experienced it, I'm sure you can at least imagine it. The tongue indeed has the power to heal and to incinerate. So even if you aren't a parent yourself, I think you'll appreciate my vantage point as the one having to referee these situations.

Whether you're dealing with boys or girls, you can commiserate in the shared experience of navigating the torrents of illogical communication with a small human who is still growing a prefrontal cortex. If you weren't a science major, the prefrontal cortex, located in the frontal lobe, is the slowest part of the brain to mature and is responsible for things like controlling coordination, understanding future consequences, developing language skills, and—most worthy of note here—regulating emotion.[1] I think hospitals should send every firstborn home with a onesie that reads, "Be patient with me. I'm growing a frontal lobe." When things go off the rails in my house, I constantly mutter to myself, *Relax, Mike. Prefrontal cortex. Prefrontal cortex. They don't have a brain yet. At least, they don't have all of their brain yet.*

That's just the beginning of what makes discourse with daughters so challenging. Although males take even longer to develop their prefrontal cortices, plentiful studies suggest that female brains process emotion differently. So, while there can be some misguided generalization here when it comes to emotion, science actually finds increased activity in more brain regions for females.[2] That means, if it seems like your daughters feel their feelings more intensely, it's not just you. It's their brains. Neurologically speaking, women have "more" emotion than men. As a male, I found it necessary to understand this to make sense of my world. Women are aware of more of their emotions than I am. This is significant.

I have four female children. My wife is a female. My dog is a female. The estrogen levels in our house are through the roof. In response, I've developed some helpful practices. Most days, I repeat a mantra over and over: *I will not escalate when they escalate. I will not escalate when they escalate. I will remain calm when they lose their minds. I will not escalate when they escalate . . .*

I've recently concluded that doing or saying the same thing over and over while expecting a different result is indeed the definition of insanity . . . and parenting. But we must. Whether parenting boys or girls, we parents must not only reinforce basic truths to our children, but we must also remain calm even while our kids are being completely unreasonable. To me, this forced endurance gives parents a seeming edge in disagreeable conversations. If we learn to embrace our children when they're flailing, we'll be better equipped to talk to anyone.

Nothing will prepare you for arguing with adults like arguing with children. That is, if you take the time to kneel down on their level and learn how.

Let me give you a small example. We recently allowed our two older daughters to have their own bedrooms. Their whole lives they've shared a bedroom, and my wife was sensing their need for personal space. We have three bedrooms upstairs, and until recently we kept one empty as a guest room. We have a lot of guests and travelers come through our house, so we like to have that space open.

We sat our two oldest down to explain the situation. "We're going to give you your own rooms, but here's the deal. When your grandparents come into town, or when someone else comes to stay, one of you will have to give up your room for a couple of days so we have space. Can you be okay with that?"

"Oh, yes, dearest father!" they sang in unison. "We shall be most generous with the space you have lavished on us. It shall bring us no small amount of joy to adhere to your most reasonable yet simple request. As you have spoken, so henceforth it shall be done unto us."

One month later . . .

"Okay, girls. Our friend Mimi is coming into town, so we need one of you to give up your room and sleep on the cot."

Release the kraken!

Utter chaos broke forth like fury from heaven. Lightning bolts burst from their eyes. Their faces exploded into hysteric flames as they consumed both my wife and me with their indignation. "THAT'S NOT FAIR! HOW DARE YOU MAKE US SLEEP ON A COT! IT'S HORRIBLE! IT'S INHUMANE! YOU TREAT US LIKE HOMELESS CHILDREN ON THE STREET!" I'm not kidding about that last part. My ten-year-old legitimately said that, to my shock and horror. I bit my tongue so hard it almost bled. Keeping your mouth shut is no small task when an adult is hurling insults at you, but when it's your child screaming, it seems to take an even more colossal effort to hold it together. It's one thing to shut up when your opponent is following what seems to be a neuro-pathway-resembling logic, but when logic leaves the building, it's hard to hold back. It also seems the smaller the human, and the less reasonable the debate, the greater the fury.

THREE RULES FOR CHILDREN . . . AND ADULTS

Before I tell you the rest of that story, I want to share a bit about what my wife and I have been learning lately when it comes to our parenting—namely, *when you have kids, you must learn to bend or you will break*. Remember all that stuff about holding the tension? It's inconveniently true. In the times I think I should hold the line, I usually find what my kids need is to have me absorb the tantrums that cross over the line. It can feel like I'm not being the authority they need. But remember, this isn't a book about simply winning arguments. It's about cultivating spaces of listening and grace. To do that, my wife and I try to follow three simple rules that have been helpful for us. They've changed how we engage not only with our daughters but also with the entire world.

1. NEVER SEND THEM AWAY
I want to start by saying there are undoubtedly parenting books that say the exact opposite of what I've concluded, so read on here

with a big old heaping pinch of salt. Again, I could be wrong, but we don't do time-outs anymore. We used to. We would tell our daughters to work it out alone until they could be reasonable. But we started to find that isolation had a way of fostering shame, allowing it to creep into the spaces that solitary confinement creates. We also realized we were communicating to them that certain behaviors would cause us to push them away. We concluded that when our daughters raged, they needed to be pulled in close, not cast out. We don't restrain them or anything. They're free to go as they please, and they do. Occasionally, we do add qualifiers. We might ask them, "Could you step into the other room while you're screaming? You're welcome here if you lower the volume a bit. We want to be able to hear what each other's saying." They will stomp out of the room sometimes, but we no longer send them away.

Science is backing us up on this. Research is beginning to reveal that children with either too little or too much cortisol have cognitive impairments later in life.[3] To put it simply, when we don't allow our children to feel their feelings, they learn to squash or dismiss them. Sound familiar? As a result, their bodies can never escape the fight-or-flight mode of their limbic systems—the part of the brain professionals refer to as the "lizard brain."[4] The lizard-brain part doesn't make assessments reasonably. It just tells you to run, fight, or freeze. When our children are kept in this state of panic, they can't follow the natural progression of emotion that results in self-regulation.

"Stop it! Put a lid on it." That's what too many of us were told our whole lives. Early on in our own parenting, my wife and I unknowingly sent our daughters the same signals. We began worrying that we were telling them that they were too much. Sadly, it's sort of a self-repeating cycle. It's the message we received as kids, so we keep the loop going with our kids. What's more, I've found that I usually want my girls to put a lid on it most when we're in public. Maybe it isn't their behavior that needs to change. Maybe I need to worry less about being embarrassed by them and more worried about being with them. My wife and I no longer send them away, because we want to stop the cycle.

Notice I'm advocating to never send them away. That doesn't mean that sometimes I don't need to remove myself from the room for a moment. Sometimes to gain our composure, we must exit and breathe before we can reenter the fray. Taking a step away is an entirely different thing from sending someone away. Can you see how this trickles down into how we interact with the rest of the world? The more I'm able to sit with my daughters in their tantrums, the better I am equipped to sit with adults in theirs. What would our discussions look like if we at least tried to stay in the room with one another?

2. NEVER RAISE YOUR VOICE

My wife and I have a goal of never raising our voices with our children. Full disclosure here: We do raise our voices. A lot. Well, I should say I do. My wife is much better at restraint in this area than I am. It's something I'm slowly making progress in. I've realized that I most often raise my voice when I don't feel like I can take the time to listen and be listened to. I want it to be quick and easy. Time is the most aggravating of demands when it comes to arguments, especially with kids. Our time is a precious resource, so we are dangerously protective of it in ways we don't even realize.

Think about it: If your goal is to keep your voice low, you can't shout over your kids. If you can't shout them into silence and you can't send them away, you'll have to wait for the silence to come.

With my children this could take hours. I'm not kidding. There are times it has taken hours. If your opponent is raging, you must bide your time to remain in conversation. It's so hard to get to that point. It requires time and demands a different posture. We are constantly practicing kneeling down and looking our kids in the eyes. Standing above and lording over them might seem like an easy fix, but it doesn't address the root of the issue.

I really believe every child flails because deep down they're asking the big questions: *Am I too much? Are you going to love me if I push all your buttons?* I'm not saying we shouldn't stand firm and make clear lines. I'm saying we must be firm and confident. And if I really think about it, I realize that raging back at my children usually comes out of my own fears and frustrations. The more at peace I am within myself, the more peace I have to offer them. A great question to keep asking ourselves is, *Am I reacting or responding?* When we stay calm in the middle of the fray, it radically changes the environment in our home. This is true with all my relationships, not just with my children.

My brother-in-law Kris recently mentioned something that made me think. He said, "We always want our kids to quit weeping and wailing, but our kids go crazy with us because they trust us. The crazier our kids are when they speak to us might actually be a sign of how safe they feel. It's when they bottle it all up that we should start worrying." Our girls' teachers have told us similar things. The kids who are the most out of control in the classroom are usually the ones who can never explode at home. Shockingly, all our daughters are incredibly well behaved at school. Their teachers tell us that makes sense. The pressure builds until it finds a way out. If kids learn it isn't safe to explode at home, they'll learn to do it elsewhere.

Maybe this isn't something you've considered, but do you find people in your life let loose around you, or is everyone carefully calculated and well-behaved? When I don't raise my voice, I give others permission to use theirs. I want to become that safe place where my friends feel like they can be, as my sister's band croons, "all kinds of emotional."[5] I understand that's a delightful thing to pontificate about but terribly inconvenient when all you want is for your child to *just stop crying*. However, peace that is achieved by walking through the storm together is quite different from a false calm held in place by a heavy fist. That's not walking in peace. That's a standstill. And that is true for all relationships.

3. DISCIPLINE IN LOVE

"Discipline in love" is not the same thing as "Don't discipline when you're angry." Don't get me wrong; not disciplining in anger is a good start. But it's not what we're aiming for. More than merely disciplining when I'm not angry, I want to wait until I'm disciplining from a real place of love. This is a higher aim, and ought it not be all of ours? We don't aim to keep peace. We aim to make peace. That's a world of difference.

We parents would do well to remember our hope for our discipline *before* we engage. If God disciplines those He loves (see Hebrews 12:5–11), then so must we. I hope you also notice I'm not saying we let our children rule. We don't let them rage in any way they want either. We let them feel, and we let ourselves feel with them. Maybe it's a bit redundant, but when I engage in debate with adults, am I considering this basic essential aim with my children? Is the goal of this interaction to love? Am I looking to love or merely looking to win?

BACK TO THE BATTLE

Let's rewind to the moment with my daughters and the sharing-of-the-room debacle. As soon as my two eldest began screaming, I turned around to slip out of the room. My wife called to me from the other side of the room, "Hey, we're not leaving, right?"

Instead of immediately doing a one-eighty, I slowly kept rotating until I was facing her again. *She's right. She's right,* I had to remind myself so I didn't start to feel incensed. I stood there awkwardly listening to my wife plainly re-explain the situation to the two bellowing banshees. We let them rage for a few more minutes.

"Okay," I finally said. "Here's the deal. Your mom is right. Your rooms are a gift. In our family we set a high importance on hospitality. That means we don't believe we're blessed so we can keep it all to ourselves. We're blessed so we can bless others. If you can't view your rooms as a gift to share, we'll remove the privilege from you."

"YOU'RE GOING TO KICK US OUT OF THE HOUSE?" my daughter screamed in disbelief.

"No, sweet girls, I didn't say that. I meant we'll have you go back to sharing a room so we can keep a room empty to share with our friends and family." I patted myself on the back for such a marvelous construction of reason and charity. My daughters were less impressed.

"That's just great! This is the worst day of my entire life! I'm not sharing!" My ten-year-old stormed off and up the stairs. My twelve-year-old sat there crying hysterically.

My wife and I shared an exhausted look of "You got this." I waited a few minutes and then went up to where our younger child was lying in her bed. "No! I don't want you." She rolled over and buried her face in her pillow.

I sat down beside her bed and gently stroked her back. "I just want you to know you're never too much. I understand how hard this is. We love you and we're here. I'm so proud of you and so glad you're my daughter. We'd love to keep talking when you're ready."

I walked downstairs and collapsed on the edge of our bed. Haggard, I looked at my wife. "Being a bad parent would be so much easier."

A few moments later, both daughters were back in the bed with my wife, giggling at photos on her phone. They had both apologized to us, and each said they wanted to share their room. We didn't end up forcing them or making them. We held the line, but it was a flexible one.

NEVER EASY, ALWAYS WORTH IT

If you can find the grace to remain loving as you listen, you'll be amazed at how well your kids can regulate on their own. I do want you to know this is not always the way it goes. Obviously these are aims, not guarantees. But it can go this way sometimes. There really is a way to remain calm, and there's a way to more lovingly disagree.

If we can learn to do it with our children—who are scientifically proven to be more unreasonable than most adults—then surely we can learn how to lean in, stay steady, and disagree in love with anyone. Or as I like to say, if we can peacefully remain in conflict with children, maybe we can make peace with anyone.

We don't always have to double down; we can learn to dance. Isn't that more like the heart of God? We are His kids, aren't we? And how do we talk to Him? And what is His heart toward His kids when they do? Even when we're insensible and moaning and full of absurdly unreasonable petition? His heart is *gentle and lowly*. He is *slow to anger*. He is *rich in love*. That's what the Scriptures remind us over and over. His heart is patient. Plain and simple, He listens different. His ears can suffer longer and can take much more abuse than ours can. Romans 2:4 says that He changes us with His kindness. His kindness is the catalyst to our repentance. If that's the case, then it's worth wondering, why would we try to change anyone's mind through any other means than what our God uses to change our hearts? The answer to this question is where we start finding grace in the gray.

10

Talking to God, Talking to People (and Sometimes, Opossums)

The function of prayer is not to influence God, but rather to change the nature of the one who prays.

—Søren Kierkegaard

Nothing will change how we talk to people like changing how we talk to God. My friend John O'Brien is a prime example. He is one of the most gracious debaters I've ever met. He also has one of the longest fuses of anyone I know. It's strange because he wasn't always that way. Things began to change for him when he started to change the way he prayed.

When we first met, John was a bit of a hothead. He'll even tell you he was a bit of a meathead. He loved the gym and theological sparring. He still loves a good didactic row, particularly when it comes to the Reformation. But somewhere along the way, his tone experienced a dramatic shift. I think it happened when he started talking to opossums.

I don't know if he still talks to opossums, but he did.

To be precise, he prayed to an opossum. To be more precise, he prayed to God . . . through an opossum.

Yes. John is both gracious and a tad bit crazy.

Now that you're undoubtedly confused, let me give some context.

When I was in my early twenties and interning at the large South Florida community church called Christ Fellowship (the one I mentioned in chapter 2 when talking about Michael Neale), I lived in the intern house just a half mile or so from the back of the church building. There was a large field of undeveloped land between the church and our house. A makeshift dirt road, where the maintenance vehicles would drive back and forth, connected our lowly intern house with the church offices. I'd walk to church most days and consequently began to grow quite fond of this lonely patch of wilderness amid the suburban sprawl of Palm Beach Gardens.

This is the field where I would truly learn how to pray. This several-acre backyard is where I learned to converse with the Almighty. I know that sounds strange, but it's true. I never had a robust prayer life in high school or even in college. To be completely transparent, I still wrestle with my attention span and often find my mind turning to grocery lists or descending into sleep during many of my prayer times. (I had a friend once encourage me, "What better compliment to give your heavenly Father than falling asleep in His lap." Hope that helps you stop beating yourself up too. You're welcome.)

But one morning, after finding myself drooling all over my bedroom floor after another failed attempt at isolated immobile meditation, I decided to kick the dust around the field and see if simply walking and talking would help me pray for more than five seconds at a time. Little did I know that I would wear a path around that old field over the next two years. It became a haven for me. It was my sacred space to holler at the heavens. It was the place I would sit on the roof of my car at sunset and scream my questions to the sky. It was the place I made a picnic for my first date with my future wife. It also became the space where I sobbed for hours after she broke up with me. If I'd known we'd get back together and have four children, I probably would have sobbed a little less. Maybe.

Regardless, it worked.

As I walked and vented and walked and vented, I found that simply walking led to a revolutionary evolution in my attention span. I started prayer walking every morning and, after a while, every night. Nighttime was when the magic happened. The shadows of palm trees cast by moonlight have an eerily spectral quality to them, and they beckoned me into the fuzzy thickness where the space between God and man feels thin.

Then I began to invite my roommates to pray with me. This is where John comes in.

I know you might be thinking, *Wow, you guys sure knew how to party.* And I'd have to say, you're right—we got all the feels and none of the hangover. It wasn't a bad practice, was it? And I know it was crazy awkward the first time I asked some of the guys to join me: "Hey, you guys. I know you're about to watch *The Lord of the Rings* straight through for the fifth time, but I was thinking we could go walk around the field and pray together instead. What do you think?"

To my great shock, most of them agreed. "Sure. I've got ten minutes to kill." I wouldn't say we were overwhelmed with desire for God, but I think we were just unsatisfied enough with everything else that we kept showing up. We would meander together but apart, filling the empty field under the moon, trying to learn from one another.

One night a few of us were walking and praying. Out of the corner of my eye, under the dim light of a crescent moon, I could just make out the shape of John. He was crouched low, still as a slug. I watched him as I walked. He didn't shift or slouch. He was absolutely transfixed . . . a human statue. After thirty minutes or so, the few of us who were walking the field and praying began to trickle back into the house. All of us except John.

A full hour later, John finally came through the front door. We were all more than a bit curious as to what had held his attention for so long. Certain he had just encountered the Holy Spirit in some utterly profound way, I beseeched him, "John, tell us what you heard! What did you see? What did God reveal to you?"

"It was . . . an opossum," John said, wistful and starry-eyed.

"A what?" I choked back a laugh and asked again. "For real, bro, what did you see?"

"I told you already. I saw an opossum and he saw me."

"Well," I started, "I'm sure he saw you, but what were you doing looking at an opossum for so long?"

"I was praying to him," John said, serious as death. "Well, not to him, per se," he explained. "That would be blasphemy. I was praying to God through him."

"Wow." I couldn't figure out if he was messing with me, so I proceeded cautiously but with amusement. "What did he say to you?"

John blinked twice and twitched reflexively. "He said nothing, but he stared into my soul. Of that, I am certain. I had a feeling the Lord was looking at me through his opossum eyes. I began to think of Balaam's donkey, so I spoke thus unto the vermin, 'Fair opossum! If thou hast a message from the Lord, be it far from me to cause you to tarry. I am His humble servant, and I am listening!'"

"Sooo . . ." I was fighting back a series of stifled laughing fits by now. "Did you hear anything?"

"No," John said, looking more than a bit forlorn. "But at least I gave God the opportunity. You never know how He's going to speak or who He's going to use."

You never know how God will speak or who He's going to use. I will never forget the wisdom of John and his opossum.

PRAYER UNFILTERED

Unfiltered expectancy changes everything when we pray. It changes everything about how we discourse. It changes everything about how we disagree.

I saw this play out with my friend. When he began getting more unfiltered with his prayer life, it led him to a more expectant posture in every other area of his life. Most of us would quickly disdain any directive in our head that would say, "Listen to the opossum." That's quite fair. It is ridiculous. But for John, I can look back to this "ridiculousness" and see God crafting a new spirit within him.

The more unfiltered and the more expectant we get when we talk to God, the more we will start to expect to find Him in others. The more we expect He'll use something or someone as unlikely as an opossum, the more we will keep our ears open to unexpected people. But just like making space on our calendars to meet in a field and pray, we must make space in our souls to meet with God.

Some of us are a far cry from expecting to hear from God through others because we're still too entirely filtered by our own thoughts. I'll try to unpack that a bit. You see, it took a year of my walking that field and venting my prayers to God before I ever learned to get still enough to hear from Him. You might not be wired that way. Maybe stillness comes naturally to you; not to me. I've found that I can only begin to hear the whispering voice of God after I've spewed out all of my thoughts first. Like letting my kids rage so they can regulate, I have to prayer purge all the concerns in my head before I can find the calm to listen. I find it terribly intriguing that Psalm 62:8 directs us to "trust in him at all times, O people; pour out your heart before him; God is a refuge for us. Selah." Refuge and trust come after pouring out our hearts.

I guess you could say it like this: A full-vent prayer to God clears the way for listening. If your head and your heart are full of hammering concerns, they must be poured out before new thoughts can enter. I suppose this is why Paul says, "Do not be anxious about anything, but in everything by prayer and supplication with thanksgiving let your requests be made known to God. And the peace of God, which surpasses all understanding, will guard your hearts and your minds in Christ Jesus" (Philippians 4:6–7). We pour out so God can pour in. Let your requests be made! Get unfiltered. Yes, let your supplications be accompanied with thanksgiving, but pour those prayers out so His peace can enter the space left behind.

I wonder what kind of screening process we bring to our prayers. I think God wants to do that for us. If we bring the whole orange, maybe He removes the pulp. But we try it the other way around. We think He needs our help, but it's we who need His. *Pour out your hearts before the Lord.* He's encouraging us to bring prayers that are unfiltered. He knows all our thoughts anyway, right? Yes, we're told to take our thoughts captive, but how do we even know what they are if we don't speak them first to God? When we realize this, it frees us up to vomit out all that's in our hearts to God.

This creates vulnerability. It's amazing how humbling it is to hear what's going on inside of us when we have the courage to speak it. In turn, it allows us to offer the grace for others to come unfiltered too. This is a bit of a secret hack in regard to disagreement. Like our children sensing they're never too much, when people sense they can come with unfiltered thoughts and language, they can relax. They speak more candidly, more vulnerably. They relax. We relax. And when we do, we find more grace and space in those moments than we had before. I wonder how many of us are constantly editing our adversaries because we're constantly editing ourselves.

My friend John went on to lead multiple Bible studies in various prisons and penitentiaries all over South Florida. He's been doing that for the last twenty years now. I think it's clear that he learned to expect that God's voice will come from anyone. You could say that unfiltered prayers lead to unfiltered conversations with people, which leads to unfiltered experiences with God. John expects God to speak to him through a marsupial. That's a guy who doesn't look down on anyone or anything. This is really my point. John is one of the most well-read and well-thought-through theologians I've ever met.* John knows more than most on theological treatises, major historical church councils, and systematic theology in general. And yet, when he debates with someone, he is one of the kindest and the least argumentative people I've ever

---

* Whatever theological position you hold, I guarantee you John not only knows it but has also read several books about it. Well, at least 75 percent of several books. This is a bit of an inside joke, but if you flip through any book in his personal library, there's a very good chance you'll see intense and expansive highlighting in several different colors on almost every line of every page until you get three-quarters of the way through. Then you'll see nothing. John will tell you, "Usually by that point the authors are repeating themselves."

witnessed. He isn't a pushover either. Despite being a hothead in his earlier life, now he is anything but. I firmly hold that the reason John can debate with so much kindness and empathy is because he knows how to pray. He would add, "He who has been forgiven much loves much."

The more we understand our forgiveness, the more unfiltered and ridiculous our prayers are permitted to become. The more we assess ourselves honestly and pour out our every grievance, fear, and concern at the feet of the Almighty, the more space we are left with—space we can step into where we feel less triggered, a selah space where others can join us. It's a space where we can wait. It's a space where we're less defensive and more expectant. It's a space where we anticipate hearing from God Himself possibly through the words or actions of another person, even when we think the other person is a bit of an opossum.

EVERYTHING'S NOT AWESOME

People who pray unfiltered have space. They have a peaceful space to share with others. When I believe God gives me permission to pray everything to Him, I'm correspondingly able to give God permission to say anything to me. A space opens between us. There's a space to praise but also a space to lament. I assure you it's true. I say this often: Prayer is more like a space maker than a request punch list. The more I make room for God to disagree with me, the more I give others the permission to do the same. The more I expect to hear God's voice, even from the body of an opossum, the more I expect to hear wisdom from God through unlikely sources. And paradoxically, the more of my anger I share with God, the more grace I'm given for others when they are angry. The more disappointment I cast on the Father, the better I'm equipped to share sadness with someone else. I see myself in the reflection that prayer creates.

Have you ever experienced this? You don't realize how ridiculous some of what you're feeling is until you speak it out in your prayer closet. When we take time to hear ourselves, we hear others better. The more frustration I pour out on God, the less I need to pour out my aggression on others. The more I realize how wild and frantic my thoughts really are, the more gracious I'll be when I hear what sounds like a wild and unfounded argument.

It's crazy how turned around we've made it. We lament to our friends while offering dishonest, perfect prayers to God. It ought to be the other way around. God wants all of our prayers. The praise, the thanks, and the laments. I learned this from my friend Jason. He's a pastor in Indiana and is more well-read than any of my friends—even more than my friend John, come to think of it.* Jason pointed out to me once that there are generally three types of psalms in the Bible. There are psalms of praise, which generally sound like "Everything is awesome!" Then there are psalms of thanksgiving, which go something like "Everything was not awesome, but now everything is awesome." Then there are psalms of lament. Those sound like "Nothing is awesome. O God, will it ever be awesome?"

Shockingly, there are more lament songs than any other type in the book of Psalms. Why, then, do we not see this connection to our lives? To have a robust relationship with God, we must direct our laments to Him. We cannot constantly filter our prayers and imagine we won't unfairly filter people as well. Ironically, most of

---

* Unlike John, Jason reads his books all the way through to the end.

us complain to one another while neutralizing our aggression toward God. Maybe it's supposed to be the other way around. Let God have it all. He's the only one who can take it.

Sadly, many of us grew up bottling and monitoring the words and attitudes we brought to God. We learned to tamp down our rage, and as a result, that rage comes out on others. We pounce on any misspeak we hear around us. It's like all our disappointment and desire have to come out somewhere. What if God is the safest person to fully vent on? What if we got it all out of our systems with Him, so much so that it changed the way we interact with others? We think we can just box it up and lock it away, but it almost always comes out somewhere and at someone and in ways we never intended.

Now, if all this sounds a bit foreign to you, I invite you to try it. Would you consider giving yourself a week of unrestricted prayer? Explore the lament side of your prayer life. Pour out your heart to God. Let Him have it all. Hold nothing back. I'm not sure what you'll find on the other side, but I bet you'll find a calm after the storm. Who knows? You might find yourself as still as John, watching an opossum in a field.

It's worked for me. When I throw all my hurt and questions on God instead of on others, I seem to come out on the other side like a city street after a cleansing summer storm. The smell of a refreshing rain is in the air, and the oil stains have been washed away. It reframes my words to everyone around me. After I hurl everything at Jehovah Jireh, He provides me with a new narrative to approach others with. When He gently affirms, "You're not too much. You are My child," it makes me want to come to others like that. I want to have a running banner in my brain that says, "You're not too much. You're God's child."

THE WAY WE TALK TO GOD CHANGES THE WAY WE TALK TO PEOPLE

Jesus said, "Truly I tell you, unless you change and become like little children, you will never enter the kingdom of heaven" (Matthew 18:3, NIV). By this, I think Jesus was commending the beautiful innocence, humility, and dependence of kids. It makes me think of the sweet prayers my daughters prayed when they were little. There was no pretense, just the purity of little hearts and minds. We are born with unfiltered expectancy. Our filtered skepticism is learned.

It's a strange polarity that I've seen play out time and time again, as evidenced by reading through my journal. When I've been less honest with God, the more guarded and antagonistic I've been with others. By contrast, the times I was scribbling honest, feverish prayers at God seem to be the times I was experiencing the most peace with others. This should come as no surprise. The Psalms are full of raw, uncensored petitions. It's quite liberating to draw comparisons between my prayers and some of David's more lamenting prose—and what a relief to know I'm in good company!

But it also worries me when I find myself in the company of what I call the prayerfully restrained. I'm sure you've experienced this—those times when you sit in communal prayer and find yourself listening to well-curated prayers flowing perfectly from pristine lips. When this happens, an alarm goes off in my head. *These people are not safe,* I surmise. I usually flinch and wonder when the shaken-up soda cans of their souls are going to explode. It's no wonder. We grow up saying things like "Don't say that in church," when church ought to be the place we can be the most unguarded.

This, I believe, is why Psalm 62:8 says, "Trust in him at all times, O people; pour out your heart before him; God is a refuge for us. Selah."

I've quoted this verse once before already. This time, notice three things:

1. **Trust God.** Trust His mercy and love enough to pour out everything that's in your heart before Him. Trust that He's big enough to handle the bigness of every one of your emotions.

2. **Pour out your heart.** Get unfiltered. Get raw. Get honest. This is incredibly difficult, especially for those of us who grew up in strict environments. "If you can't say something nice, don't say nothing at all," Bambi's friend Thumper's reminder echoes in our brains. While this is true with people, it needs to be just the opposite with the Lord. When you let God have it, I think you'll find He really can take it. You'll even find He's a refuge. He's a safe place to speak unbridled. David was constantly saying all kinds of outlandish things in his prayers. He said God had forgotten him forever (Psalm 22:1–2). He even blasted his enemies and ranted about how much he hated them (Psalm 139:19–22). There's plenty of debate as to why these sorts of things are included as canon, but the point is that *David was taking those feelings to the right place.* These passages are there as guideposts, showing us where to direct our bemoaning. Oftentimes, if you keep reading, you'll find David prayed a final prayer of trusting God after he'd unleashed a torrent of anger and fear in the Lord's direction (Psalm 130).

3. Selah. Rest and reflect after you pour everything at God's feet. Chances are, a deep peace will come in after the flood. There's even a chance your soul will get still enough to hear God through the unlikeliest sources.

Does that sound too good to be true? If you're really interested in cultivating grace in discourse, I encourage you to change the way you're talking to God. If you think everyone's a marsupial and you're constantly exploding with rage, try reversing the paradigm. Instead of raging at people and biting your tongue with God, try it the other way around. Talk to God the way you've been talking to people, and maybe He'll give you the peace you need to talk to those people. You might even find Him talking through the people you never could have imagined.

11

Speaking of Social Media

Never be so clever you forget to be kind.

—Taylor Swift, "Marjorie"

Nothing will challenge your ability to talk with people like social media. Notice I said talk *with* people. I say that because nowadays, social media has also made it easier than ever to only talk *at* people. It's easier than ever to speak at strangers instead of taking the time and courage to speak with them. There is no need to even feign listening in this space. Speaking is all that is required to join the fray. This is a shift from the past when the majority of our conversations were happening eye to eye. Now they're happening eye to screen. This layer of protection has provided an ever-expanding autonomy whenever we want it. Availability is increasingly controlled. We can hide behind privatized settings. We can weigh in and "peace out" easier than ever. I'm certain it has its place, but the block button can feel like the equivalent of a toddler thrusting their fingers into their ears and hollering, "LA, LA, LA, I CAN'T HEAR YOU!"

Social media has changed the game of discourse. Humans used to have to stand on an actual soapbox and address actual people if they wanted to speak into their culture. If they wanted to publish an article, they had to pass it through an editor. There was an inherent give-and-take. It was built in. I think it's fair to say that's hardly true anymore. Everyone gets a mic these days, and the ensuing noise has made it harder and harder to hear anything that doesn't immediately align with our viewpoints. The algorithms aren't helping either. The more we click on something, the more we're recommended similar views. When we're not being fed like-minded recommendations, it's usually the complaints and disappointments that receive the rest of our bandwidth.

I've been in awe of the shift. People online aren't like people in real life. There are things that have been said to me on social media that I know no human would dare say to another human being face-to-face. On social media, opinion is amplified while responsibility is diminished. We hop on. We frantically fire off zingers. We wait for our moment to dig in the knife. When confronted, we wage war or retreat to start a new fire elsewhere. The metaverse doesn't follow the same social cues. It's a battleground one minute and Ghost Town, USA, the next. It can feel like all mouths and no ears. Leave but a waft of impending controversy online and rest assured the smug monsters will pick up the scent. They'll pounce and retreat before you've even had a chance to read their rhetoric sprawled like graffiti across your comment section.

You may not share my discontent, but all of this made me want to give up on social media once and for all. Just a few years ago, I was ready to throw up a white flag. I had the towel in my hand like Rocky Balboa watching Apollo Creed. I was ready to tap out. I lamented, *Where's the hope for elegant disagreement? Is there a way to fill our comment sections with gracious conversation?* I didn't quite throw in the towel, though. Over time, I have come to believe grace in the gray of social media is possible. Tim Keller expressed it so well when he wrote, "Could at least some Christians be known for their love on the internet? And could they take part in the re-building of new spaces of public discourse in which we can pre-sent our faith confidently and listen to our critics carefully and humbly—at the same time? Yes, we could. But will we?"[1] Yes, Tim, we could. Will we? I sure hope so. I hope because I've seen it. Although, admittedly, it's been a bit of a process.

THE HARRY POTTER EXPERIENCE

I hadn't realized how different the rules of engagement had be-come in the social media sphere until one ill-fated Halloween. I was just doing my thing, talking to my followers, assuming every-one agreed with my every viewpoint, and I really hadn't detected the shift. That is, until my family dressed up as Harry Potter char-acters on the last day of October. Posting a picture of my family in wizarding paraphernalia sent many of the people who were following me into a tirade.

I hadn't anticipated this kind of reaction to what I saw as an innocent family activity. I was thoroughly shocked. I hurried to explain myself and defend my decisions. But all too quickly, I wit-nessed my online world descend into madness.

I think it's safe to say, I should have known posting that pic-ture was going to elicit some fury. If you're familiar with the ways that some Christian folks feel about Halloween—not to mention

Harry Potter—you might see the potential tension. I'd been invited to enough trunk-or-treat events to know plenty of churchgoers view Halloween as an ode to the demonic. If you find yourself thinking, *What's the big deal?* remember that in many people's eyes, I'm a *Christian* singer. Let's just say, I got to read a few days' worth of comments asking why I love Satan and want to tempt children into a life of sorcery. Naïvely, I had not expected the avalanche of concern. But as I began corresponding with hundreds of people over multiple social platforms about costumes, church history, and the origins of All Hallows' Eve, I began to grasp at the threads of the problem.

Immediately after my Harry Potter Halloween family photo post, I was unprepared for the vitriol waiting for me. But slowly, over days and weeks and eventually months, my initial consternation dissipated into tolerance. My tolerance became silence. My silence slowly grew into curiosity until finally, after years of practice, curiosity melted my heart into attentive empathy. What started as a defensive reflex eventually metamorphosized into a new purpose for my online presence. Some people picked up on what was happening. They could read the way I was listening. They read through my replies and began to write me themselves: "Wow, I don't know how you can be so gracious when they're being so mean."

"Practice," I would respond. Finding grace in the gray takes hours and hours of practice.

Now, you may not be dealing with people blasting you for promoting witchcraft, but I'm sure we could all use some practical how-tos on how to engage adversaries across the World Wide Web. Today, many of us are more present in the metaverse than we are in the actual universe. This, then, is the space where many of us will encounter the most conflict. However, when it comes to social media, this is often the place where we don't even need to go looking for a fight. Give it enough time and the fight will come to us.

WELL, THAT ESCALATED QUICKLY

I recently watched *The Social Dilemma* and *The Mitchells vs. the Machines* in quick succession. I realized that computers are indeed coming for us. I had no idea how purposefully designed many social media spaces are—they are constantly being tweaked to keep us using them. That's a tad generous. Teams are being hired to figure out ways to keep us addicted to their platforms. This means there are teams of people whose jobs depend on your increased enslavement. I hope that gives you pause.

Have you heard that anxiety is at an all-time high? I don't think it's a coincidence that anxiety is rising at the same time online media consumption is. Do you realize that you and I probably see more information in the first fifteen minutes of our day than our grandparents ingested in a month's time? My friend Carlos did a series of posts on this recently. He called it story fatigue. His point was that we are so burdened by the constant onslaught of information that we rarely pause to consider what's happening in our own hearts. Capacity is not something most of us think about when we open that one app for the fifteenth time in an hour.

Anxiety goes up and fuses grow shorter. Do you ever stop to wonder why things seem to escalate so quickly online? Does it feel like the anger you're met with doesn't match the level of offensiveness in a particular post? At the onset of my Harry Potter experience, I had begun to despair. It was the first time I had felt personally attacked online. I'd never liked being disagreed with, and quite frankly, I hated being disliked. After reading through the comments, I really figured I should give up on social media entirely. Being reprimanded by hundreds of voices at once felt like more than I could bear. I wondered how I could ever please all these followers I had amassed. How could I ever keep them all happy with me?

And then something strange happened. I had an epiphany. I wondered, *What if everyone isn't really looking to win a fight? What if all they really want is to be seen and feel heard? What if I don't need to worry about keeping the followers I've garnered but just need to keep serving them as best I can?* I know; it's not exactly rocket science. But believe me, I'm not overstating it when I tell you that my Harry Potter experience was what eventually ignited the genesis of this book.

I began testing my hypothesis. I stopped talking. I stopped typing. I started listening. I considered for the first time how vast the online universe truly is. I felt amazement creeping in. How many cultures and backgrounds and upbringings and stories were all converging at that precise moment on my channel? What began as furiously firing off links to J. K. Rowling's public professions of Christian faith slowly grew into wonder.

And then something strange happened. I realized I had finally stopped trying to win the arguments. I didn't stop having them. I just stopped trying to win them. When I was met with unreasonable escalation, I stopped throwing fuel on the fire. Instead, I started trying to understand. My friend Natalie recently marveled at me. "You just love getting in the weeds, don't you?" she playfully accused.

Of course, I thought. *There are people in there.*

I finally stopped needing to convince anyone of my opinion.

Don't misunderstand—I still wanted to convince them, but I didn't need to convince them. This is important. Instead of hammering harder, I started asking questions instead. I'm sure you've heard it enough by now, but instead of getting catty, I grew curious. I'll get to this more in the next chapter, but I changed the questions I was asking too. I did what my brother-in-law Kris calls moving from *why* and *how* to *wow*.

Why is demanding. It necessitates a reason. It's a question that puts the other person into an immediate defensive position. This does not help de-escalate at all. It does the opposite. *How* is similar. It lives in the future and puts me back in the driver's seat as the interrogator. But *wow* is different. *Wow* leans in. It commiserates. It's more like "What do you think brought you to that conclusion?" It levels the playing field so that we're no longer acting as judge and jury but engaging in a peer-to-peer conversation. And you know what I found? A gentle response *can* turn away wrath. The right kind of question can throw a blanket on what would otherwise become a brush fire.

HONOR CODE

Since we're talking how-tos, here's another tidbit I've found when it comes to grace in the metaverse. Honoring others on social media is like a cheat code for a video game. Remember that ridiculous algorithm for the title screen of the Nintendo game *Contra*? (I know I might be losing you here, but *Up, up, down, down, left, right, left, right* . . . If you know, you know.) The point is, when it comes to social media, I assure you, there is a perfect way to hack the system when it comes to disagreement. It's as simple as this:

Honor the person coming after you. In Romans 12:10 Paul says, "Love one another with brotherly affection. Outdo one another in showing honor." Outdo one another? What a weird thing for him to say. I can't think of another time that the New Testament asks us to compete with fellow believers. Here, he says, if you're going to make a competition, make it about honoring the other person.

How does honor work on the internet? I'll try to give you one small example. I posted about Novak Djokovic being detained and subsequently deported from the Australian Open because of his vaccination status. I was curious what people thought. (Okay, I was probably guilty of looking for some controversy. Let's call it research for the book.) A lady was sounding off to me, disgusted that any person for any reason would want to be unvaccinated. After several spirited exchanges with this lady, I sat quiet for a moment and considered her. I paused and tried to feel what she might be experiencing inside. Feeling prompted, I asked, "Do you feel afraid?" Admittedly, this was a bit of a left turn in our debate, but it was beautiful to practically read her countenance change in her response. Her defenses immediately dropped, and from the sound of her words, she was weeping as she responded, "I'm just so afraid." It turned out, underneath all her energy was the deep hunger to simply feel safe. Hearing this, I was moved from anger to compassion. The debate changed. I honored her humanity instead of hounding her hysteria. Tuning in to others' fears will change everything.

Have you ever read through the Gospels and marveled at the number of times the writers say Jesus "had compassion" when He looked at people? Check out Matthew 15:32 or Matthew 9:36 or Mark 6:34 or Luke 7:13 or Luke 19:41. They all talk about Jesus looking at people and being moved with compassion for them.

Jesus, unlike me, never just tolerated people. He looked at them. He saw them. He was moved by them, and that's what prompted His moving toward them. With all the ability the Holy Spirit provides, we must open our eyes to see and feel the human on the other side of the screen. As compassion rises in our hearts, honor will naturally flow from our lips. Or in matters online, it will flow from our fingertips to our keyboards.

We honor others online when we deeply consider their hearts as we engage. I'm not talking about flattery either. I'm talking about real consideration. This, sadly, usually requires more time than we can give. Often, the metrics of social media don't allow it—especially if you have a lot of followers. This hit me with new force the other day when I posted a picture of myself and simply said, "Hit me up with any questions you have. I'll do my best to answer them." Three weeks and thousands of questions and answers later, my perspective on followers changed dramatically. I suddenly felt a fresh wave of necessary repentance for all the times I thought I didn't have enough followers—for all the times I used to compare myself to other artists and lament. Now I consider how many followers are looking to me and I shake my head at the profound responsibility I possess. It turns out I already have too many followers. And chances are, so do you.

I can't tell you how many times I've gotten something like this from young artists: "How do I get more followers?"

I'll respond, "How many do you have now?"

They'll bemoan, "Only 324. I really need to boost it."

"Hmmm," I'll respond. "You know you're really crushing Jesus right now."

"What do you mean?" they ask, bewildered.

"Well, what I mean is that Jesus had only twelve followers. For all intents and purposes, you're doing way better than He was.

Maybe instead of asking for more followers, you should be asking, 'How can I honor the ones I have? How can I better serve the folks following me right now?'"

These are not the things we're usually thinking about when we check in on how many likes our video received. It might also explain why our fuses are so short. We just don't have the time to serve that many people. You might respond that Jesus had twelve disciples but regularly spoke to thousands. That's true. But my point is that He focused His energy on a much smaller group than we do. Social media doesn't have to merely be a place for being seen. I think we can turn the tables like Keller insists. We can re-create the purpose of the space, making it about showing compassion-driven honor rather than winning arguments. Flip the script. Instead of trying to be seen and gain influence, we can make it our intent to see and bestow honor.

FROM CURIOSITY TO COMPASSION

You might think I'm crazy, but go with me here for a minute. This question has kept me coming back to the internet with newfound purpose. What if we decided one of our goals for being on social media was to simply demonstrate to others how well we can disagree? This was the key for me to stay engaged. You might come to a completely different conclusion. That's great. But for me, it was a beautiful new purpose to carry through every post I created. I started asking myself, *How can I demonstrate a gracious curiosity to everyone I interact with?* Notice, I'm not saying we won't ever disagree. I'm proposing there really is a way to do it well. How do we do that? I'm still figuring it out, but here are a few more personal convictions.

When someone told me I was most assuredly going to hell because I posted a wine review online, I pinned their comment to the top of the comment section. I then replied to their comment, but not in a condescending or inflammatory way. Instead, I asked for further explanation. Otherwise, posting their comment would be the same as putting a big fat bull's-eye on their back so my allegiant followers could take them down for me.

It didn't work at first. Some quickly flew to my aid and felt it their responsibility to blast my opponent back into their living room. However, I held my tongue and my fingers, and I kept trying to faithfully reply with curiosity and credence. Where possible, I would try to legitimize an opposing viewpoint, even when it was wildly different from mine. Then, I would find another comment of someone who backed up my view and I would pin that comment too. My hope in doing so was to show others that sometimes the answer isn't so black and white and that maybe, just maybe, there are many different views on certain things. This is especially true for those things that I would consider nonessential.

It worked. (Well . . . sort of.)

After a few weeks I began to receive messages in my DMs. People noticed. They said they appreciated how I tried tackling hard things without demonizing anyone. This is particularly difficult. Nuance is exhausting, isn't it? Sifting for gold and goodness is tedious work, especially when naysayers are hurling mud at us incessantly. It makes me think of this great reminder, attributed to Andrew Carnegie: "When gold is mined, several tons of dirt must be moved to get an ounce of gold; but one doesn't go into the mine looking for dirt—one goes in looking for the gold."[2]

I guess you could say when we stop to honor someone's dissenting opinion, we simply subjectify them. It's a whole lot easier to have compassion for a person than a viewpoint. It's a whole lot harder to cancel a human when we see them as such. This is countercultural. Our culture likes to either deify or demonize people. We fuse together the person and their view—they're one and the same, and they're either all bad or all good. We label others as totally deceitful or totally trustworthy. We view celebrities as saints to be adored or as refuse to be discarded.

I think we should keep letting humans be humans. Look for the wheat. Dig for the gold instead of canceling or worshipping the source. I'd like to point out that if I void everything someone says based on their shortcomings, I'll have no one left to quote. There are plenty of authors of the Bible who could have been canceled for their indiscretions. The kingdom of God has never been a cancel culture. It is and always has been an invitation.

A PERFECT PLACE TO PRACTICE

Again, I haven't done this perfectly, but I'm learning, and I'm curious. When it comes to digital disagreements with strangers, curiosity is key. Curiosity is clutch. Curiosity is kind. These three statements have become guiding principles for me in the way that I engage social media.

Here's a fourth: Curiosity is calm. I've made a habit over the years of always waiting a bit longer than I think I should to post or reply. Curiosity keeps me calm and demands that I focus on others. If I can keep myself from knee-jerk reactions, I tend to create more calm in my channels. That might sound like common sense, but remember that the metrics advise the opposite. The metrics say that when something controversial takes place, we must comment on it as soon as humanly possible to make full use of the algorithm. Social influencers need to stay on top of what's happening in society. Weighing in fast is considered more important than weighing in well. If we want to become known and important, we've got to weigh in as quickly as possible.

Now, that might be great for driving up numbers, but I have found it to be terrible for my soul. Jumping on every trend tends to turn our whole experience into an echo chamber. It seems to me that I weigh in best when I take the time to feel the weight of the situation. When I take a few moments or even days to breathe, I tend to more fully think through what I'm going to say. When I do this, I've found my words become less exclusive and more inclusive. It also keeps me from commenting on every controversy that blows through my timeline. There are those who seem to passionately argue their perspective surrounding every conceivable current event. I have to wonder if that's what it truly looks like to be controlled by the media. I'm not always going to have the brain space or bandwidth to discuss every major news headline. That's okay. If I take time to speak to what I'm truly moved by, my words will carry more weight and wisdom. I've often found that I will write out several versions of a post or a blog and completely scrap them before coming up with the thing that I actually post. I may not be the first to the party, but at least in hindsight I'm still proud of what I contributed to it. There's nothing worse than showing up to a vegetarian get-together with a bag full of rib eyes because you didn't take the time to read the invitation correctly.

BOUNCE HOUSE

Practice patience. Practice curiosity. Practice compassion. It's all about practice. You're not always going to get it right. Lord knows, I haven't. But I'm seeing progress, and that excites me. It excites me for all of us. Maybe the social sphere doesn't have to be the perpetual bloodbath we've experienced in the past. Perhaps grace is always possible—even if grace is learning when to walk away. Sometimes wisdom is knowing when to bounce.

Sometimes the best thing we can do for everyone is to wait to weigh in. But other times, the best thing we can do is to *walk away from the fight altogether*—which might be the trickiest part of navigating the digital waters before us.

How do I determine which one to do? That's going to look different for everyone. But for me, I pay attention to the answers I get to my questions. After I ask a few exploratory questions, if someone's response reveals they have no intention of cultivating conversation at all, I know it's time to let it be. Oh, how difficult this is! It takes so much restraint to leave the fight once you've been in it a while. But I've learned to repeat this in my head: *It's okay to walk away.* After I ask my *wow* questions, I listen diligently. If I feel there's no intent to lean in with me, I let them be. I've also found it helpful to click on an individual's profile to see whether snarky comments are their typical mode of operation or not. What's especially telling is if the person has a private account that doesn't even have a name. An absent or covert moniker is usually a dead giveaway that the party you're tussling with is only there for the fight. Do yourself a favor and don't give them the satisfaction of a battle.

I love the seeming contradiction in Proverbs 26:4–5: "Answer not a fool according to his folly, lest you be like him yourself. Answer a fool according to his folly, lest he be wise in his own eyes." Remember, I know that I can play the fool sometimes. So, I have grace for the fools out there. I am one. But I take this verse to mean that I don't need to be scared to tell a fool the truth and that I also don't need to get sucked into their game.

A TROLL AROUND THE BLOCK

There's a quote I first heard from my friend KB: "Don't accept criticism from someone you wouldn't seek advice from." There's a lot of wisdom in that. The ability to receive constructive criticism from someone you trust—as opposed to destructive criticism from someone you don't—will allow you to receive critique with more objectivity and less emotional charge.

This is what taught me to stop labeling people as trolls when they attack me on the internet. While I might still call them out for trolling, that's different from calling them a troll. I'm no longer labeling people based on their dysfunction. In other words, denounce the action but not the person. Someone can be actively trolling, but that doesn't mean I have to call them a troll. It's truly remarkable how much anger this dissipates. Maybe even lean into the ridiculousness of it all sometimes. My wife knows when I'm stirring things up. "Oh, I'm just trolling around the block, babe," I'll joke.

But here's something incredibly important to consider: If the only time you feel geared up and ready to "make an impact" is when someone posts something you don't agree with, there's a good chance that you are indeed the one out trolling. It is so much better for kingdom building when we remain focused on what we are endorsing and building up instead of what we are intent on tearing down! I'm sure you've heard it said before, but it bears repeating. What a mighty thing it would be if we were known for what we were for and not what we are against.

This, I believe, ought to be what sets up a Christian to hold a unique amount of grace in online spaces. Hopefully, we aren't merely building our brands but building the kingdom. Hopefully we aren't desperately accruing followers out of a fear of scarcity but serving our followers out of an overflow of abundance. Hopefully, we can and will be the ones to "present our faith confidently and listen to our critics carefully and humbly—at the same time." It's possible. I'm telling you. There is an abundance of grace in the gray, especially in the digital realm, if we remember there's a real human on the other side of that comment. There's a real human who may simply need the honor and compassion that we've first received from the Lord. If we've been loved at our worst, perhaps this is a perfect opportunity to love others at theirs. So much more than the most eloquent prose we could ever post, those are, I believe, the most important things we'll ever share.

12

Feelings Are Our Friends

Listen to your own voice, your own soul. Too many people listen to the noise of the world, instead of themselves.

—Leon Brown

I f we don't know what's going on inside ourselves, how can we ever hope to understand what's going on in others? If we're going to make space to listen to what's really happening in one another's hearts, in person or online, first we're going to have to do the work of listening to ourselves. If we're ever going to learn elegant discussion with strangers and our friends, we must first learn to understand what things trigger our own hearts. In short, we'll have to make friends with our feelings.

That might be difficult to imagine, since many of us spend our energy discounting what we feel. If you grew up in the church like I did, this might even sound completely counterintuitive. Looking back, I feel like the message I received in Christian contexts was to only ever listen to my faith and not ever to dare learn to make friends with my feelings. I was taught to consider all my feelings as enemies: *"Distrust feelings at all costs. Your heart is out to get you, so don't dare trust anything in there. After all, the heart is 'deceitful' and 'desperately wicked' (Jeremiah 17:9,* NKJV*), so we aren't supposed to trust our hearts. We're supposed to* tell *our hearts what to feel! Remember, #FaithOverFeelings!"*

Excuse me if I go a bit Wreck-It Ralph here. But if I see another meme telling me to have faith over my feelings, I will break the entire internet. Okay. That's dramatic, but I do have strong feelings about feelings, if you didn't catch that yet. I especially have feelings about how they align with faith. You might be thinking, *Why? I thought faith over feelings was exactly right! If I have to trust one over the other, I choose faith. My feelings have made terrible captains for my soul, and my heart has led me into some pretty dark places.* I get that. You're right. Feelings alone can never guide your faith, but faith without feelings is like a sailboat without wind. Feelings are gifts from God that make life worth living. They're the wind in the sails. Hopefully faith tells us which way to throw the sails and direct the rudder. Besides, if you don't know what your heart is feeling, how do you know which promises to steer it toward? I hope I can quickly unpack this new perspective for you.

First, I want you to know that feelings are not to be feared and discounted. Rather, they are meant to be gifts that we listen to and learn from. If this isn't apparent, just imagine life without feelings. Imagine no tears. Sound good? Now imagine no laughter. Imagine not wanting or caring. Apathy might be the most terrifying of fates.

Second, I understand what folks are driving at when they say "Faith over feelings." True, we can't let our feelings run the show. I'm not saying that they should. They certainly can't call the shots. I get that. But while we don't always need to *act on* what our feelings are telling us, if we don't stop to name and listen to our emotions, they *will* be running the show. I've found this to be true, particularly in the realm of disagreement. Most of the gargantuan blowups I've had in my life have happened because suppressed and uninspected emotions were triggered. I've blown up on my wife and my kids at times simply because I hadn't done any inventory of what my emotions had been trying to tell me about what I needed. Therefore, if we want to hear others, we—both you and I—must learn to listen to ourselves deep down. When we don't, we try to stuff down what we feel, in the name of faith, until our feelings spill out through the cracks.

So, here's a new perspective to consider: *What if our faith and our feelings don't have to be in a constant battle?* I've come to believe that the two were never meant to be in a fight in the first place. The phrase *faith over feelings* suggests the two are at war battling for attention. But what if they were meant to be dance partners instead of warring tribes? I've come to learn that my faith and my feelings aren't competing for the pole position. I also think that it isn't my feelings' job to cancel out what I believe, and it isn't my faith's job to beat my feelings into submission.

EMOTIONAL INTELLIGENCE

What I'm beginning to describe to you here is what many researchers call *emotional intelligence*. My friend Rob Murray has two different books on the subject. He and many other therapists and researchers have made stunning observations in this realm lately. I first began learning about what my feelings were trying to tell me from the book *The Voice of the Heart* by Chip Dodd, which I strongly recommend for anyone who wants to go a bit deeper.

Let me tell you how understanding this concept played out for me. I recently joined an emotional check-in group with nine friends. Our friend Jeff Schulte assumed the role of facilitator to essentially direct the conversation. He has been a licensed therapist for decades and was therefore the right man for the job. I'll never forget how awkward the first meeting was. We sat in a circle in an empty office building. It was seven o'clock in the morning, and my coffee hadn't yet kicked in.

Jeff explained to the group that we tend to describe our emotions in complementary colors. When we describe how we feel, we'll use words like *confused* or *awkward,* but these words are really just combinations of the primary colors. I had no idea what he was talking about. *Colors?* I thought. *We feel colors? What on earth are you talking about, Jeff?*

Jeff slid a piece of paper into the middle of the circle and rattled off some words, each a different emotion: hurt, lonely, sad, anger, fear, shame, guilt, and glad.[1]

If you're like me, you're thinking, *Wow, that's a lot of negatives compared to one positive.* Chip Dodd would say that's part of the problem. We've come to label so many emotions as negative or positive instead of getting curious about what they're trying to tell us. Jeff tried to explain, "These are primary colors. If you say an emotion that's not on this list, it's probably some combination of several of these core emotions. As best you can, describe how you feel, but don't use a word that isn't on this list. Secondary emotions keep us from being vulnerable. These are the primary emotions because you feel with your heart, not with your head."

None of us really had any idea what he was saying, but we gave it a shot. We ten guys sat in a circle week after week, still groggy from a lack of sleep and parenting and all the other demands men face in their thirties, and we struggled through checking in with the emotions we were currently feeling.

"Today I feel hurt and sad and glad," I found myself mumbling in between slurps of my caffeine infusion.

"Thanks, Mike," the group chanted back. That's the other thing I should have mentioned. No one ever asks *why* you feel those things. Remember, the *why* is what puts us back into a *defend-or-dismiss* paradigm. It's what most of us have been taught to do our entire lives. We are constantly having to defend and justify why we feel what we're feeling, and if we don't have a good enough reason, we feel pressured to dismiss what we're feeling. For instance, I grew up sharing things like this in accountability groups at church. Instead of getting a thank-you for sharing, I got a mini sermon as to why I shouldn't be feeling what I just shared. Faith over feelings can keep us from learning what our emotions are trying to show us.

Does this sound familiar to you? If you said to a group, "I feel lonely and sad and glad," more often than not, you'd be met with something like "Oh man, don't be sad. Don't you know God has a plan and a purpose for your life? Don't you know God's in control? Let's be glad and rejoice! Your gladness is right. Your sadness is not!"

This emotional check-in work spilled over into my band's prayer times. We'd gather in the lounge of the bus or on the floor of our dressing room before a show. We'd read off the list and get curious with ourselves and one another. I remember walking off the bus one morning and being met by another band's tour manager—a guy who hadn't been a part of the emotional practice we had just engaged in. He genially inquired, "How we feeling today, Mike?"

Having just done the work of sorting and naming my heart's inventory, I shot back, "I'm doing well. I'm feeling sad and lonely today. Thank you so much for asking."

What did he say in response? "Oh, Mike. Don't feel that! It's a great day. We have a sold-out show. We're going to praise the Lord!"

I countered, "Well, you know, I've been away from my wife and kids for four days. If I didn't feel sad and lonely, I think something would be wrong. I think those emotions are telling me my relationships are healthy. They're telling me how much they mean to me."

Suffice it to say, that was the end of the conversation. He garbled something unintelligible and quickly scooted along in the opposite direction. He hadn't expected this kind of answer, and what I was feeling had probably triggered something like fear in him. Letting others discover their emotions can be tricky work.

WORTHY WORK

I believe discovering our emotions is worth the work. I believe emotions are a gift. All of them. Yes. Even the ones that have been labeled "negative." Feelings are windows to our souls. They are like messages in a bottle. They call out to us, hoping we lean in and listen to what's going on behind them. They can be quite insightful friends if you give them permission to speak.

For instance, what if I told you that anger is your soul wanting something?

What if sadness is your soul letting you know that something mattered?

What if loneliness is a gift letting you know that you were made for community?

What if guilt is letting you know you need to own your mistake and apologize?

On and on it goes. Lean in long enough and you might be shocked at what you find.

I know this might be difficult to consider, especially if you're thinking about what might happen if you let your emotions take over. Let me assure you, that's not what I'm advocating. Yes, if we listen solely to our feelings, we won't ever know which way to go. There's always a move we can make. One way goes toward health; the other goes toward unhealth. Leave emotions unattended and they'll drive us straight into elevated confrontation. But on the flip side, if we never get curious about what they're trying to tell us, things will eventually come out sideways. Properly inspected and listened to, our emotions will let us know why someone's words in our comment section affected us so dramatically.

So now, what if instead of saying "Faith over feelings," we said "Feelings informed by faith"? Or what about "Faith informed by feelings"?

I know, it's not nearly as bumper-sticker worthy and may even require some explanation. Let me try. If emotions weren't gifts from God, why did He hardwire us with them? If we weren't supposed to give credence to our feelings, why would the Bible tell us about Jesus's feelings? Jesus wept at a friend's grave, didn't He? Why would Jesus cry over Lazarus unless sadness itself was some sort of gift? Think about it. He was about to raise him from the dead, after all. What's the point of crying? Jesus cried tears of blood in the garden. On the cross, He begged and questioned, "Why?" And yet, I don't think we would say Jesus let His feelings get the best of Him. Rather, when He felt, His faith informed His feelings. His feelings informed His faith. He went on to raise Lazarus back to life. He surrendered His will to the Father. He stayed on the cross. Remember, Jesus felt it before He fixed it. Maybe we can too.

In 1 Thessalonians 4:13, Paul indicates that although we grieve, we don't grieve like those "who have no hope."

Do you see?

He doesn't imply that we don't grieve at all.

He says that when we grieve, our grieving is different.

We grieve, but not like those with no hope.

Our grief has changed.

The sadness remains, but our despair has been removed.

Hope and grief dance together.

We don't bow down and surrender to our feelings.

But we don't coldly defeat or dismiss our feelings either.

If our faith and our feelings aren't meant to be enemies but dance partners, then the sadness and the hope are meant to float together. They aren't divorced. They don't need to be. They're meant to be in a marriage. In a healthy relationship, our faith talks to our feelings, and our feelings talk to our faith. They inform each other. This is what it is to be human. Body and soul, faith and feelings; we are complicated things.

For too long, my feelings felt too complicated to bother deciphering. This has all been changing for me lately as I've begun studying emotions and how to have intelligence about what they're communicating to me—like hurt telling me I care about what a friend thinks of me or anger telling me I want something to change. If I listen to what I feel, then I begin to understand how I should act. I begin to see where faith is telling my feelings to go. Changing the way I listen to my heart alters the steps I take. It also radically shifts how I listen to others.

When my daughters are too scared to go upstairs, I don't scream, "STOP FEELING AFRAID!" They can't do that. What I say is, "Are you feeling afraid? Good. Now you have the opportunity to have courage." If you weren't afraid, you'd simply be naïve. When the Scriptures exclaim, "Do not be afraid," they cannot mean "Don't ever feel fear." The feeling is not under our control, but our response is. Maybe what Scripture means is something more like "Even though you feel that, you don't have to be paralyzed by it." Your heart is not the dictator, but neither is your mind. There's more to the story than what you feel in this moment, and there might be more to the story *behind* what you feel in this moment. Move through. "Do the next right thing," as *Frozen II* reminds us. Let the faith inform the feeling; let your choices be the result of both.

ALWAYS INVITATIONAL

Now, let me inject some nuance here. In our check-in circle, after I shared and the group said thank you, Jeff asked me a different question: "All right, Mike, what's behind some of those things?" Maybe it's just semantics, but do you feel the invitation in those words—more so than if he had just asked *why*? The idea is that each emotion is a doorway and behind each doorway lies a whole world to explore. Before we board up the doorway, we should take a peek inside and find out what's there.

After Jeff's inquiry I took a second to think. Then I answered, "Hmmm. Well, I'm sad because my wife and I had a misunderstanding last night. I'm a bit lonely because I've been on the road and I'm feeling disconnected from my friends here in town. I guess I'm feeling unknown by the guys in this circle that I'm trying to make connections with. But I'm glad I'm here, because now I have the opportunity to be known."

The guys looked at me intently. They had just been given the gift of hearing where I really was and what was really going on inside me. It's incredible how deeply connected we feel when we let ourselves be known.

A few beats of silence and then Jeff prodded. "What do you need and want, Mike?"

"What?" I sort of half responded, caught in a bit of delirium after becoming so vulnerable with the group.

Jeff directed me. "That was a lot to share with the group. You obviously want *something* to share that. What do you want to ask us?" Jeff has a Jedi-like way of cutting to the quick of what you're longing for before you even know it yourself.

"I guess, well . . . I was wondering if anybody wanted to grab coffee after this. I could use a friend right now." Hands quickly shot up—a nod and a wink from my friends to remind me that I was not alone in how I was feeling.

Feelings informed by faith. Faith informed by feelings. I invited them both so I could invite others to show up too.

Do you see what happened? I'll just pick on my loneliness here so you can see the point. We don't want to admit we're lonely. We feel like it's admitting some lack in us. *I should be fine being alone. I have Jesus after all, right?* Instead of listening to our loneliness, we just dump some shame on top of it. But when I stop and listen, my loneliness is actually yelling at me because I need something. What do I need? At that moment, I needed some community, which isn't ever something to be ashamed of, is it? Aren't we all made in the image of a communal triune God? Why on earth should we ever be fearful to admit we need another person? But if I stuff my feelings down and don't acknowledge them, I don't know what I'm needing, so I don't know what I need to ask for. I end up feeling numb, and when you numb your feelings long enough, things tend to come out in ways we don't want. Most of my worst arguments have been the result of unknown and suppressed emotions. I

numb them, I discount them, and I push them down, until someone unknowingly trips the wire.

LOWER THE BASEMENT TO RAISE THE ROOF

Here's one of my favorite verses to reinforce this point. Psalm
126:5 says, "Those who sow in tears shall reap with shouts of joy."
Okay, I grew up thinking this verse was about praying hard enough
for what you want and then God having to give it to you. If you
cry and weep and sow, you will reap and receive and have joy.
After a few conversations with Jeff, I no longer believe that's the
case. Now I believe what the psalmist is trying to tell us is *don't numb
it down*. We think happiness comes from turning off our sadness.
That simply isn't the case. To sow in tears means we have to feel
the full extent of our sadness. We need to let the basement go
lower instead of stifling our tears. To feel the full extent of joy—or
to raise the roof, as we like to say—we must be willing to feel the
weight of our sorrow as well. Lower the basement to raise the roof.
Sow in tears and reap the joy. If we don't, we will not only raise up
sadness by dismissing it but also bring down the roof of our joy,
squashing ourselves like Luke Skywalker in the trash compactor.
We'll numb our feelings until life squeezes them out in unhealthy
ways.

This is terrifying at first, because what if we go into our sadness and never come out of it? Strangely, I've found that's rarely
the case. Depression can be the result of a lot of different factors,
but often it is more likely to emerge from our desire to discount or
avoid our feelings than from our curiosity to understand them.
The more we explore feelings like hurt and sadness, the more the
ceiling of joy can rise. Joy and gladness have a way of increasing

when we're willing to open up to feelings like hurt and sadness. Sow in tears and you will reap with shouts of joy.

How are you going to listen to a friend sitting across from you if you can't learn to listen to the emotions happening inside you? I know this might sound like a radical shift, depending on your upbringing. But hear me. At the risk of redundancy, I'm not saying your emotions are always right and you always have to do what they're telling you. I'm saying you should always pause to listen to what's going on inside you before you address what happens outside you. I'm saying that if you learn to listen to your emotions, you can decide what to do with them. And hopefully, you'll learn how to build real empathy with others.

DON'T MISS OUT

Think again on the loneliness I named in my circle of friends. If I had stuffed it down and dismissed it, I would have missed what I really wanted and needed in that moment. And I would have missed the chance to ask my friends to come around me. That's the key. With every emotion we name, we're given an opportunity to move toward health or unhealth. I could stuff loneliness down and let it drive me further into isolation, or I could recognize it, name it, and—as it turned out—let it lead me into reaching out for friendship.

What do you want?

What do you need?

Until we let our feelings have a seat at the table of our soul, we won't ever learn to give a seat to the people disagreeing with us either. I've seen it over and over and over. The more I defend or dismiss the feelings I have inside, the more I tend to unnecessarily battle the people around me. The grace I have for everyone lessens. My feelings need my faith—not to cancel them but to interpret them. Does that make sense? My faith is meant to be more like an interpreter than a scriptwriter. "What I'm hearing you say is . . ." "Are you suggesting . . . ?" My faith keeps questioning my feelings until they come to a mutual understanding. That's the point of this whole chapter and why it's important to include. Oftentimes we assume we know what someone is trying to say to us instead of trying to deepen our understanding. We do this because we often assume we know what we ourselves are feeling instead of going deeper and listening longer.

I can't help but get excited for some of you reading this. You've been so busy making enemies out of your feelings, you didn't even realize there was another option. Perhaps if you can learn to make friends with something as complicated as your feelings, you might even learn to make friends with the people who have only ever frustrated you.

Grace in Faith and Deconstruction

In essentials, unity; in non-essentials, liberty; in all things, charity.

—Marco Antonio de Dominis

In a sermon in 1809, Thomas Campbell said, "Where the Scriptures speak, we speak; and where the Scriptures are silent, we are silent."[1] This is beautiful insight. It amazes me that two hundred years later we still need to be reminded that there are some things worth arguing about and some things that aren't. Two hundred years later, we're still building unnecessary theologies where we'd do better to awe at the mystery. Not that conjecturing is bad, though. We discuss and we ruminate, but still we struggle to know when to speak and when to remain silent. This is an incredibly difficult task. We're all trying to figure out what's immovable and what's not. What is paramount and what is dispensable? It's oddly encouraging to find that this was apparently a problem two thousand years ago as well—hence the reason we find this in Titus 3:9:

"Avoid foolish controversies, genealogies, dissensions, and quarrels about the law, for they are unprofitable and worthless."

In the epigraph above, Marco Antonio de Dominis seems to be sounding a bell, calling us back from the unnecessary controversies we dive headlong into. Yes, we want to be unified in the essentials and free in the nonessentials, but of course, this leads us to ask, "What are the essentials?" and "Who decides what they are?" Great questions. I'm not sure I have all the answers, but I'll offer a few thoughts.

I think folks in faith circles don't realize how quickly they needlessly pull so many of their beliefs into the essential category, when they'd do better to leave them in the gray. Could it be that some of our differences are really preferences, traditions, or particular interpretations? Could it be we're constantly adding to what is really necessary? Ask yourself. Have you ever stepped back and written out what you believe and whether it's absolutely essential or not?

You might be wondering what my answer would be. Well, if you really want to put my feet to the fire, I'd say that I'm an Apostles' Creed kind of guy. I think it cuts away the fat and centers on the nonnegotiables quite nicely. In case you're unfamiliar, here it is:

I believe in God, the Father almighty,
maker of heaven and earth;

And in Jesus Christ his only Son our Lord;
who was conceived by the Holy Ghost,
born of the Virgin Mary,
suffered under Pontius Pilate,
was crucified, dead, and buried.
He descended into hell.

The third day he rose again from the dead.
He ascended into heaven,
and sitteth on the right hand of God the Father almighty.
From thence he shall come to judge the quick and the
dead.

I believe in the Holy Ghost,
the holy catholic Church,
the communion of saints,
the forgiveness of sins,
the resurrection of the body,
and the life everlasting. Amen.[2]

For me, anything outside this creed is not in the essential realm of my faith. You might disagree, but per the theme of this book, maybe we can talk about it in a grace-filled manner? As you can see, it's pretty concise. It certainly isn't overly exhaustive. Some might say it's lacking. What about you? Your head is quite likely buzzing with many other doctrinal positions and clarifications that seem to be missing.

When it comes to faith, it amazes me how much disagreement is a difference not really of *belief* but of *interpretation*. Within a lot of church circles, if you have an argument about certain doctrinal tenets, many will quickly condemn you, saying things like "You don't believe the Bible!" In reality, the rub ought to be stated this way: "You don't believe in the same interpretation of that scripture as I do."

Notice the disparity. We tend to grossly distort our incongruities when it comes to the Bible. I guess that should come as no surprise. Talking about emotions is one thing. They come and go, ebb and flow, and are essentially subjective. On the other hand, for most of us, faith is about objective truths that bear eternal implications. It would make sense that in these disagreements, things escalate quickly.

So, how do we lovingly disagree when we talk about what we believe about God?

It's a crucial question. A. W. Tozer argued it's the most important one. In his work *The Knowledge of the Holy*, he said, "What comes into our minds when we think about God is the most important thing about us."[3] That's strong language, and I think he's right. Who we believe God to be colors the way we see and interpret everything. But if we're all looking at the world through different-shaded "God glasses," how on earth are we going to agree on what we're looking at? It's been said that Jesus is a many-sided jewel.[4] Depending on which side you're looking at, you will unknowingly exaggerate one aspect of Him over the others. Do we all do that? With more than forty-five thousand denominations of Christendom in the world,[5] I would say the answer is a glaring yes.

If you've studied the Enneagram at all, you know there is a belief that people are wired differently at a very deep level. For example, certain people are wired to emphasize correctness, while others are drawn to mystery. Could it be we're all wired to call attention to a different side of the jewel that is Jesus? I shouldn't have to tell you, but that would seriously affect our interpretations of Scripture—and everyday life, really. Before you dismiss me, saying, "Oh, not more personality-type stuff," I ask you only to consider this: Acknowledging a friend's differing inner motivations might help you have a little more grace for them and for yourself. After all, one of the most unrelenting admonitions in all of Scripture is a call to be unified.

I can list a few verses in case you don't believe me:

- "I in them and you in me—so that they may be brought to complete unity." (John 17:23, NIV)

- "Make every effort to keep the unity of the Spirit through the bond of peace." (Ephesians 4:3, NIV)

- "I appeal to you, brothers and sisters, in the name of our Lord Jesus Christ, that all of you agree with one another in what you say and that there be no divisions among you, but that you be perfectly united in mind and thought." (1 Corinthians 1:10, NIV)

Similar admonitions exist in Philippians 2:2; 1 Timothy 1:5–7; 1 John 2:9–11; 1 Thessalonians 3:11–13; and Matthew 5:9, to name a few.

We are called to be unified. It is glaringly obvious. But how? And why aren't we? Why do we feel this insatiable need to draw lines and divisions? Could it be that we draw them in unnecessary places? Could it be we forget not everyone has the same personality we do? Could we remember we all bring a bias to the Bible whether we realize it or not? I know certain lines need to be drawn to even know what we're unifying around . . . but forty-five thousand. Can we all agree that we've gone a bit overboard? I know that might be unnerving for some. As an Enneagram Four, I swim a little easier in the waters of mystery than others. So maybe it's unfair of me to ask. But when do we admit we haven't allowed the gray of God to exist anywhere in our theology? Remember, we must hold the tension between two truths.

How do we accomplish unity with all our differing perspectives and personalities? It's fascinating to me that when Paul is describing how the church will "attain to the unity of the faith" in Ephesians 4:13, he precedes it by describing the five types of leaders God has implemented to accomplish this. Verses 11–13 say, "He gave the apostles, the prophets, the evangelists, the shepherds and teachers, to equip the saints for the work of ministry, for building up the body of Christ, until we all attain to the unity of the faith."

God is a genius. Look at this move He made. Apostles, prophets, evangelists, shepherds, and teachers are never going to be focused on the same things, are they? Could it be that's the point? I'd even argue that more often than not, they will be sharply opposed to one another. An apostle will be thinking about vision. A prophet will be thinking about revelation. A shepherd will be thinking about the people. An evangelist will be centered on salvation, while a teacher will be focused on doctrine. Why in the world would God do that? Why would He purposefully force such differing personalities to be smashed together into tension-filled unity? I can't say for sure, but it seems that He knows it's the only way to figure out what's essential and what isn't.

It's quite revealing to ask, "Does your church welcome these five kinds of leaders?" Most churches I've been in don't have room for this kind of divergence. Most have room for a shepherd and a teacher, tops. But apostles and prophets are labeled as weirdos, and the evangelists are usually out on the road.

My friend Chuck is a pastor who advises church staffs. He pointed this out to me the other day and simply asked why it's so hard to keep five people like this around all the time. I have to wonder, *What would happen if these five people were constantly calling one another out?* Perhaps it would force the congregation to double down on essentials while learning to dance in the gray. Could we possibly see a new unity spring out of that five-person wrestling match? What's more, would we find it easier to "have mercy on those who doubt," like Jude 22 insists?

Let's explore that.

DECONSTRUCTING DECONSTRUCTION

What do you do when someone doesn't just have a different opinion about some tenet of faith but has turned their back on their faith altogether? Some people say we're in the middle of a deconstruction movement—that many people are walking away from the faith they've publicly professed. And it's not just everyday people in the pews walking away either. It's all kinds of pastors. Every day I see another TikTok of an "exvangelical" testifying to how they espoused what they now believe is "stupidity." We've even seen high-profile pastors and worship leaders, Christian authors and musicians dramatically change what they believe about God. Some of these are people I've never met, while some have been dear friends. For some of us, hearing these stories can feel like having our bedcovers ripped off in the middle of the night. We go from cozy to shivering in one fell swoop. We feel betrayed, disillusioned. It's difficult to deal with this kind of cold, because often these people were the same ones who tucked us into a warm bed of faith every night. So how do we respond? What do we say?

When it comes to responding to a friend in the throes of deconstruction, some people think we need to double down even harder on black and white. I've heard many argue that the more grace or gray we give "these sheep in wolves' clothing," the more space we give the Enemy to lead the young and naïve astray. I understand that concern, but in my experience, we usually err on the side of too little grace, not too much. What if, by trying to draw harder lines, we end up laying stumbling blocks across the path to Jesus? Paul says in 1 Corinthians 1:23 that "Christ cruci-fied" is "a stumbling block." That tells me I need to let Jesus be the one to trip them up, not me. I don't need to create any more ob-stacles on their way to Jesus.

So, how much mercy should we give those who doubt? Let me try to answer this with one of my all-time favorite and often overlooked scriptures: "The Lord's servant must not be quarrel-some but kind to everyone, able to teach, patiently enduring evil, correcting his opponents with gentleness. God may perhaps grant them repentance leading to a knowledge of the truth" (2 Timothy 2:24–25).

All right. Let's break this down for a minute. These verses are likely to be far more important than all the other words I've writ-ten in this book. If you're going to talk about God, if you're going to correct opponents, if you're ever going to achieve unity while giving merciful space to the doubts people have, Paul tells Timo-thy, you must not be doing so from a quarrelsome place. "The Lord's servant must not be quarrelsome." *Ouch. Rewind the tape.* I need to sit with that for a moment. I think we all do. When I talk about God, am I starting from a quarrelsome place? How much of my desire to correct someone who is questioning their faith is really fueled by my own secret desire to be seen as someone who knows the right answers? Scripture warns against this compulsion. We don't correct just because we like the attention. We don't cor-rect to gain influence. We don't speak up because we like sounding smart. We correct because we deeply care about the person.

I cannot stress this enough. When we engage in debate over matters of belief, we must constantly check in with ourselves. *What place am I coming from? Am I talking to this person because I care about them or because I want a notch on my salvation belt? Do I want to love, or do I simply want to win?* I think you'll find this one thought alone will address hundreds of areas that could use a few more shades of gray.

Let's go on.

You must be *kind to everyone.*

Stop. Read it again. Whom do I need to be kind to? Oh, right. *Everyone.*

Paul reinforces this in Romans 2:4: "God's kindness is meant to lead you to repentance." I've already pointed this out, but I'm going to keep saying it until it sticks. If God changes people through kindness, why do I think I can do so differently? What motivation am I using to change others? Please don't gloss over this.

Next in the 2 Timothy passage? Paul says be *able to teach.*

Whoof. I believe we teach best when we speak from what we deeply know. Teachers at universities typically teach in their areas of expertise. If you're a biology professor, you probably won't be giving a lecture on Shakespeare. That's worth noting. Unfortunately, social media proliferation has given lots of folks the opportunity to position themselves as teachers in areas where they might not be qualified. In James 3:1, the Bible warns that teachers will be judged more strictly than others. That ought to give us pause. *Do I really have the wisdom to speak to this?* It also ought to give us some relief. Not only can I remain silent on nonessentials, but maybe I would also do better to keep my mouth shut in areas I don't really understand. Before we jump on our soapboxes and attack someone for their beliefs, it might be worth pausing to ask ourselves, *Am I the right person to speak to this?* Frankly, I've realized that some arguments are above my pay grade, so to speak. In those areas, maybe I should let someone else handle it. It's also a relief that sometimes we can simply say, "I don't know." Remember the four magic words: "I could be wrong." Sometimes, the best three words to follow those up with are "I don't know."

What else did you tell us in the 2 Timothy verses, Paul?

Patiently endure evil.

Ooookaaay.

In today's knee-jerk defamatory culture, that bit is laughable. Endure evil? And do it patiently? I'll be the first to say I don't like evil, I don't like enduring it, and I especially don't like enduring it patiently. That's something about God that drives me crazy. I don't like it when I think He's enduring the evil of others, but I love it when I realize that's how He handles me. He is absurdly patient with us all. Let that soak in before you try to teach anyone about anything.

Now here's the last bit, and I believe it's the kicker. Paul says when you correct someone, do so *with gentleness*. We could just camp out there, but it gets even better. Then "God may perhaps"—*perhaps!* I love that word there!—"grant them repentance." Wait. God grants repentance? *God* changes them? If that's true, then we must realize that *we* don't.

Okay, let's recap:

Not quarrelsome.

Kind to everyone.

Able to teach what I'm talking about.

Patiently endure evil.

Correct gently.

Perhaps God.

I don't discount there has been a mass exit from the evangelical church of late. What confounds me about this, though, is that many of the people I've talked with about their leaving the church have expressed their departure didn't center around their questions as much as how their questions were handled. Many also express a radical change in their views about the role of the church and how it operates, but not about Jesus. I've even thought about starting a conference called "I Love Jesus but I Fell Out of Love with the Church." That's probably a bit long to put on a flyer, but you see my point.

The bad news about the good news is that everyone gets to come just as they are, so that means the church is constantly full of folks who are in process. Sometimes I wonder if we really believe Jesus is able to call people to Himself. I can't help but think that some must believe He can't do so without us. I've said this before, and I'll say it again until I'm blue in the face: God is not counting on you. He's *inviting* you into what He's already doing. I believe if you get this, it will completely change how you debate about Him with others.

Not long ago, my friend, who was the lead singer of a Christian band, posted a picture of himself with a caption explaining that he'd undergone a dramatic examination of his beliefs. Let's call it a reinterpretation. He did not think he believed many of the things he formerly had espoused. What he had not expected was Fox News running a front-page story on him the next day. Unfortunately, the feedback in the comment section wasn't what I would describe as patient, kind, gentle, or non-quarrelsome. The word that comes to mind is *crusadish*.

"What's wrong with today's Christians?" some bemoaned. "This is why liberals cannot be trusted!"

Others lamented, "You're destined to hell for your questions! You're leading others astray!" And some asked, "If you don't believe in God, then why are you preaching to us about it?"

I pondered.

The fact that men and women who were once quite public about their belief in Jesus could reach a place where they question everything should not come as a great shock. Believing in Jesus is hard. It's really hard. In Mark 10:25–27, Jesus called faith in Him humanly impossible. It's as impossible as a camel going through a needle. When we take a hard look at the world, questions abound. We must honor real questions instead of dismissing them. *How can a good God allow genocide, homicide, child slavery, sickness, sex trafficking, famine, war, death, and every other unthinkable atrocity that fills the news every day?* Who wouldn't agree that evidence against the existence of a good God is at least reasonable if not justifiable? It's no wonder Paul says in 1 Timothy 3:9, "They must hold the mystery of the faith with a clear conscience."

Mystery. Let's not breeze over that word. If we're ever going to find grace in nonessentials and deconstruction, we will have to make friends with mystery.

Remember, Jesus said, "You search the Scriptures . . . yet you refuse to come to me" (John 5:39–40). God is not a problem to be solved but a mystery to encounter.

It's why the Hebrews called Him "holy." The original word is *qadosh.* It means, among other things, "set apart."[6] In some sense, the most important thing to know about God is that He's far greater and more mysterious than what you can ever know. Mind blown.

THE HEAVENLY WRESTLING MATCH

Since *Israel* means "wrestles with God," then to be in God's kingdom means, among other things, that you've been invited into a divine wrestling match with Him. That's how close He wants us. He wants us to bring Him all our questions, all our doubts, all our fascination and fears. Just as I said earlier when I talked about prayer, God not only is able to handle our questions, but He also tells us to pour them out on Him.

"Jesus isn't fragile," my friend Chris reminds me. Jesus isn't after the regurgitation of dogma; He's after our sweat and our tears. He wants us. He wants the real us, even the struggling parts of us. Even the parts of us with more questions than answers. Maybe He especially wants those parts. He wants us to wrestle with Him, which means He wants us face-to-face. Wrestling is ear to ear, arms in arms, kicking and rolling and ugly and intimate. Sometimes the wrestling leaves us with a dislocated hip (à la Jacob in Genesis 32:25). That's okay. The limp lets others know we've been with God.

Words aren't enough. All those scriptures the Pharisees had memorized were not the end, in and of themselves, but merely signposts pointing to an encounter with Him. He is the end goal. He is not a system of thought or a dogma to recite. He is a person. It's why I wrote a song years ago entitled "The Truth Is Who You Are." If that's true, then it stands to reason that He is after not just the correct regurgitation of facts about Him but also an actual encounter with Him. This, more than anything I've told you, gives me remarkably more patience with those who say they don't believe anymore. Questioning faith doesn't scare me if Jesus is a person. If He was merely a belief system, it would absolutely terrify me. He isn't. This one audacious passage in John 5 allows my nervous system to relax. The Scriptures are not God. They point us to a meeting with Him.

In John 1, John calls Jesus the *Logos* (translated as "Word" in English), and many have misinterpreted that to mean Jesus is the

Bible. Most commentators refute that understanding, though. When John says "Logos," he's saying Jesus is the "meaning behind everything."[7] Jesus affirmed in John 5 that He is not the Bible. The Bible points to Him. It makes sense, then, that He would go on to tell the crowds in John 6 to eat Him and drink Him, leaving many disheartened and confused. He is a person, not a belief system.

WEEDS AND WHEAT

Jesus told us His kingdom is not like the ones this world constructs. His kingdom is not a witch hunt. It's more like a rescue mission.

It's not a team.

It's not even a country club.

It's a body.

It's a living organism.

This is illuminating. Body parts don't work the same way and don't even serve the same function. I would never think that my eye has the same vantage point as my foot. This tells me we are to consider one another's perspectives instead of wasting energy canceling them out.

However, in the same breath, I think the body analogy gives us a better understanding of the pain we feel when some defect. It can feel like losing an arm or a leg. Brothers and sisters are parts of our own body. It's why it hurts so badly when they say they no longer believe. But losing our own legs and arms is very different from losing a debate, and our posture should reflect this, shouldn't it? I think keeping this in mind will remind us to not cut off folks who question their faith but instead pull them closer. After all, some who deconstruct will eventually reconstruct with a stronger faith than they had before, won't they? Well, that's the hope anyway. Remember what it says at the end of Revelation: "The Spirit and the Bride say, 'Come'" (22:17). "Come" is not "Good riddance; we didn't need you anyway."

One of my favorite stories Jesus ever told was the parable about the landowner with a field full of wheat. When I think of debating fellow Jesus followers or those who consider themselves ex-followers, this parable in Matthew 13 looms large in my mind. Let me recount it in my own words.

Jesus says an enemy comes along and plants weeds overnight in the farmer's field. When the weeds start pushing their way up between the wheat stalks, the farmer's workers are eager to dig them out. "We got this, boss!" I imagine them saying. "We are really good at tearing out weeds."

"Hold it right there," the landowner in the story responds. "Leave the weeds where they are. If you go around pulling out all the weeds, you're going to tear out all the wheat along with it. I'm sorry, guys, but weed pulling is not your job."

So, then, what is our job? you might be asking. *If it isn't to identify the weeds and tear them out from among us, what's our job in this agricultural analogy?*

I don't want to add to the story here, but can I offer this? Differentiating between weeds and wheat is a gray area. As followers, we don't know who's who. As Jesus teaches, our job isn't to determine who is a weed and who is wheat. If I'm reading this right, I think our job is to whisper invitation to them all. Instead of standing before the fields scolding them for their lack of fruit, what if we bent low and got our knees dirty? Maybe our job is to treat everyone like they're wheat until they finally believe it for themselves. Maybe we don't need to obsess over who's in and who's out. Maybe we get to treat everyone like they're in until they finally come home. In the fields of Jesus's kingdom, we welcome the weeds into the wheat and invite everyone to the party. We don't lock the gates and require a secret handshake to get in.

In the same chapter, Jesus also said the kingdom is like a farmer throwing some seeds around everywhere. The farmer actually seems wasteful as he tosses them haphazardly about the path. (I wonder what kind he was throwing. Mustard seeds, perhaps?) The seeds scatter all over the place, and eventually the plants grow. But some wither. Some get trampled on. Some are strangled, while some thrive to impossible heights. Some are eaten by the birds. I don't know about you, but I don't want to help the birds swallow seeds off the fallow ground. I want to work with the gardener, watering the soil. However troublesome a plant looks, I want to be in the business of repairing and reviving. I think we—myself included—should leave the pruning to God.

When I think about these parables, I remember what my evangelist friend Jeremy once told me. He said these parables remind him that every time he speaks, his job looks a little different. His job is to take part in reaping God's harvest. But there are stages to that, aren't there? One waters while another plants. Sometimes one's job is merely walking through a field and taking out the rocks. Sometimes the person gets to gather, but sometimes they're tending, never knowing if it's weeds or wheat they're speaking to. In other words, one person doesn't have to do it all.

I want to encourage my brothers and sisters to worry less and believe in God a little more. He is the one who causes the seeds to sprout from the dark places. He brings the rain. He causes the sun to shine. He doesn't need the workers, but He invites us to participate in His harvest. Sure, we debate. We are prepared with the reasons that we believe. We avoid quarreling for quarreling's sake. But at the end of the day, we aren't pulling out weeds or eating the seeds that haven't grown yet. We wait. We bear with one another, and we trust that God is the one who ultimately illuminates Himself to His people. This ought to fill our arguments with a newfound patience, endurance, and kindness.

Perhaps.

Perhaps.

Perhaps.

Perhaps God will grant them repentance.

You might be wringing your hands as you read this. *What are you saying, Mike? When are you going to outline which beliefs are essential and which are nonessential?* Don't you realize? I already have. What if the way we disagree is essential? Paul says we must not be quarrelsome. Be kind to everyone. We must patiently endure evil while speaking the truth with all gentleness. Maybe that means the essentials are things like kindness and patience and love. From what I deduce from the Apostles' Creed, the essential is Jesus. What if that's enough?

Maybe all I'm saying is we Christians should stop freaking out.

Did you hear that? Stop. Freaking. Out.

Quit freaking out on the believer who turns unbeliever.

Quit freaking out on the unbeliever turned believer in something else.

I don't think anyone's really an unbeliever anyway. We're all believing something. Perhaps God will bring them back around.

I know this is a blow to the old ego, but God can take care of Himself, can't He? He isn't rattled. He isn't unsettled. He knows we are just dust (Psalm 103:14). And the arguments? I think it's safe to say He's heard them all before, which means I'm only ever speaking up for a God who has already been speaking to people's hearts. I'm still convinced, after all my years on this planet, most people aren't won to Jesus because of an impressive argument. And most don't leave the church because of a theory. More often than not, it's wounds from the insiders that cause them to run out the doors of the church and not look back. So, quit freaking out. Stop pulling up the weeds. You might just go pulling up the wheat along with it.

Isaiah puts it so poignantly: "A bruised reed he will not break, and a faintly burning wick he will not quench; he will faithfully bring forth justice" (42:3).

We need to allow others' faith to bend. My friend Gabby once commented, "If your faith can't bend, it'll break."

Perfectly stated.

Let's not break the bruised reeds among us. Let's not make it our job to quench the flickering flames of faith among the harsh winds of life. God doesn't.

Though we may not applaud others' belief systems or the routes they're taking, we can at least applaud their attempts at being honest with themselves and others. I'm sure of this much: None of us get closer to Jesus by pretending to be something we're not. I know the gray areas and doubts can be unsettling, but removing the pretense is the first step toward Him. Even if we end up taking the long way around.

14

Who Is Your Samaritan?

Common sense is nothing more than a deposit of prejudices laid down in the mind before you reach eighteen.

—Albert Einstein

Nowadays people often use the phrase *good Samaritan* to describe someone going out of their way to do something good: "I got my car stuck in a snowdrift, but a good Samaritan came along and pushed me out." "I was choking on a steak, but a good Samaritan knew the Heimlich maneuver and helped me hack it out." "I was running from a pack of zombies, but a good Samaritan pulled me to safety." We've all said that, right? I joke, but even stranger than that idea is that we've missed Jesus's point. I believe our current use of the term *good Samaritan* is quite the opposite of what Jesus was trying to say.

You might be familiar with the basic bones of the parable, but let me summarize it quickly. (Check out Luke 10 if you'd like to read it yourself.)

A lawyer asked Jesus, "Who is my neighbor?" Jesus did what

Jesus always does and seemingly avoided the question. He told a story instead. In it, a man was jumped and robbed on a dangerous and winding road, an eighteen-mile journey that descended more than three thousand feet,[1] between Jerusalem and Jericho.

The people originally listening to Jesus tell this story were very familiar with the road and the inherent dangers it held. The journey between these cities was tedious. Way stations were set along the way as temporary stopping places for travelers. Plenty of riff-raff also lurked about, waiting to do exactly what they did in Jesus's story—attack a traveler and take their stuff. In the parable, a priest was the first on the scene. He ignored the injured traveler, and then a Levite did the same. They both passed the man and did not dare help him. Then, Jesus threw a serious curveball to His listeners. He explained that after the religious leaders took turns passing the hapless victim by, a Samaritan man came to his aid. The Samaritan tended to the injured man and even ended up paying his hospital bills.

This was shocking. And not for the reasons you might think. Jesus wasn't telling a story to marvel at the goodness of the Samaritan, although the man's mercy is applaudable. Jesus was telling a story about the indwelling prejudices that keep us from seeing certain people as good in the first place. Jesus's story was provocative not because of what the Samaritan did but because of who he was. That a Samaritan, of all people, would be the helper in the narrative would have shaken Jesus's listeners profoundly. The Jewish religious elites would have been absolutely flabbergasted. After all, Jews and Samaritans hated each other. Devout Jews considered Samaritans a lower class of people altogether.

You can imagine the discomfort of the Jewish audience when Jesus asked, "Who was this man's neighbor?"

The lawyer couldn't even bring himself to say "Samaritan." He merely grumbled, "The one who showed him mercy" (Luke 10:37).

By making the hero a Samaritan, Jesus was pointing a finger straight at the ingrained racism of the crowd. He was telling a story about prejudice. You could probably even title this parable "The Discriminated-Against Samaritan"—although, admittedly, that doesn't flow off the tongue. But it is nevertheless a story urging all of us to have compassion for all people, regardless of race or religion or other differences. It's a story about the way we write off "those kinds of people." It's a parable about teaching our brains to overcome our subconscious biases and see our "neighbor" as anyone who is in need.

What's more, if we read the story in the right context, it also instructs us how to have a more gracious disagreement. Think about it. If we're ever going to hear one another out, we must strip away the labels we slap on those who don't agree with us. If we assume there's nothing good in the person we're talking to, we'll be hard-pressed to hear them out. Jesus was indicting the temptation we all feel to write off the people who don't think or look or sound like us or aren't enough like us to deserve a place in our stories.

I have to wonder.

Could it be that Jesus's story wasn't really just a story?

What if the story of the good Samaritan was really meant to be a question?

I mean, that would be Jesus's style, wouldn't it?

A lawyer asks Him, "Who is my neighbor?"

Jesus responds with, "Who isn't?"

It's classic Jesus, and it's as culturally important as ever.

Prejudice is a timeless problem.

SAMARITANS NOW

A few thousand years later, we are still grappling with the implication of this parable. Let me ask you the question this way: Who is *your* Samaritan?

What do you mean by that, Mike? Well, whom do you think you get to write off? I know you probably wouldn't ever think you're doing that, but sit with it for a minute. Who do you think couldn't possibly have a sound argument to contribute? Which news station is full of liars? Which movement doesn't have a leg to stand on? Who isn't worthy of a chance to speak?

I believe Jesus is asking us to take a little emotional inventory. Prejudice is often subconscious because we're seldom aware of the discriminatory mindsets we've inherited. Like Einstein pointed out, "Common sense is nothing more than a deposit of prejudices laid down in the mind before you reach eighteen."[2] Prejudice is like humidity in the air. It just seeps in.

So, let me ask my question another way. Who do you think God would never use? Who do you think He shouldn't use? Who do you think is unfit to carry God's goodness into the world? Who do you automatically tune out the second they start talking?

You might think this is a reach, but I think it's directly on the nose. One of the most identifying features of Jesus's ministry was His ever-expanding invitation of salvation. After all, His inclusiveness is a large part of what got Him killed. Read in Luke 4 when He quoted Isaiah 61 in the synagogue. The reason everyone wanted to murder Him afterward is because He talked about the prophets helping Gentiles.

To put it a bit more bluntly, I believe that if Jesus told this parable to white people in Mississippi in the 1950s, He would have identified the Samaritan as a Black person. If He told this story during the 2016 Republican primaries, the Samaritan would have been Hillary Clinton. To a Ukrainian, maybe the hero is a Russian. I want to be sensitive here, but hopefully you see my point. Jesus was telling them, and He is certainly telling us, that God's goodness can show up in and through anyone at any time. If that's the case, then discrimination has no place in the kingdom. We become the people who are willing to listen to anyone. There is no one we write off. We expect to hear Him through friends and even those who were formerly our enemies. There's no one off-limits to Him. If that's the case, then we ought to feel squarely challenged to consider whom Jesus could have put in the story that would offend us.

Who is my Samaritan? Who is yours? Maybe it's someone from a different religion. Maybe for you, Jesus would have made the Samaritan a trans person. Maybe it's a straight person. How differently would you respond to this parable if the man who helped was an alt-right conservative or a far-left liberal? What if your Samaritan is someone in the church who hurt you?

Pick your poison. About whom have you unknowingly told yourself, *There is no way Jesus could ever live in or work through them!* I want to challenge you in this chapter: Don't ever let yourself fall into the trap the Pharisees did. It is my ardent belief God can use and speak through anyone He pleases. It's also my belief that we become much more disagreeable in the places we stop looking for Him.

My friend Justin McRoberts recently mused online that relationships are built by our committing to each other, not by our coming to the same conclusions. I love this reevaluation. We must resist writing off anyone. We can be radically different but still radically committed. Thank God He doesn't write us off but rather rewrites us into His story. It turns out, Jesus loves to expand our narrow view of where we think He'll show up next.

MY BROTHER'S BROKEN HEART

A few years ago, just a few days after Christmas, my own unknown prejudices were brought to the surface in a way I had never expected. My brother's broken heart broke mine.

I was preparing to hop in my car and drive to a Cru conference in Indianapolis. Indianapolis is just four and a half hours from Nashville, so I was making a quick overnight trip. The conference planner had asked me to come and speak, then follow my talk with an hour-long acoustic concert. I jumped at the chance. I love speaking to and performing for college students. With the excitement and possibilities of early adulthood coursing through their brains and veins, there are few spaces that are quite as electric for communicating.

Snow flurries were beginning to drift through the late-morning Tennessee air, and I was tossing my things into the back of my car, hoping to beat the weather up to Indiana. Just before I closed the trunk, my brother called from inside, "You mind if I come?"

I was surprised he volunteered to join me. To be transparent, we haven't always been close—due mostly to our seven-year age gap. And at this point, we'd never been tight. So, after I'd said at our family brunch that I had to drive up to Indianapolis, I was quite surprised my brother jumped at the opportunity to invite himself on the trip.

He ran home and packed a bag. Within the hour we were driving cautiously through the unexpected snowfall up Interstate 65. On the drive, I was both surprised and pleased to find we were quickly engaging in some of the most honest conversation we had had in quite some time. Squinting through the now-blizzard-like precipitation cascading down the windshield, I said, "Man, it's so good to be talking like this. I have to say, John, I've wanted to be closer to you for years, but for some reason I've kind of felt like you were being somewhat resistant. I don't know; it definitely could just be in my head, but has there been a wall up between us? Maybe I helped build it? Maybe I'm making that up?"

"Well, not exactly," he said. "It's just . . . well . . . years ago, a lot of your fans started finding me on social media and condemning me. They told me I was a disappointment. They told me I was going to hell. I didn't really know what to do, so I just thought it would be better if I kept my distance."

"Oooh." I mused for a moment, trying to keep the white lines in sight as the wind swirled the snow across the road. I searched for what to say next, landing on, "Because you wanted to protect yourself?"

A contorted look spread across his face. "Me? No, of course not. I can handle it. I was trying to protect your career."

"Ooooh," I said.

Growing up, I didn't know my brother was same-sex attracted. He came out openly about it only in the last decade. In terms of our relationship, it's still a bit of a new development. And let me not mince words here: It has, at times, been a tumultuous one. Like so many others who had a similar Christian education and upbringing, my brother was placed in the sharp minority, decidedly so, because of his sexual leaning. It's fair to say, he didn't exactly feel free to discuss what he was feeling. You could even say he was treated like a Samaritan. If I can be vulnerable here, I'm sure I hurt him in ways I don't think I'll ever quite understand. My buddies and I didn't know what he was feeling, so we would constantly make gay jokes to one another in front of him. We didn't know what we were saying, but I'm now keenly aware that is not an excuse—not only for his sake but for all people with differing sexual attractions and identities. I'd like to say I never meant any harm by it, but today, the thought of my complete ignorance and lack of empathy causes my skin to crawl. I've wept over the isolation and fear I know my brother experienced at my hands and my words.

What did he do when he first began to recognize those attractions in himself? It breaks my heart to know that I took part in unknowingly pushing him away. By his own account, he often felt neglected, singled out, discriminated against, and abused. *Jesus, forgive me.* Without even knowing it, my actions and my attitude labeled my brother a Samaritan.

I debated about whether to include this story in the book. But if my relationship with my brother can be something like a case study to learn from, I'll sleep a little better tonight knowing you might learn from my mistakes. I certainly don't have the expertise to go on a deep dive into human sexuality, nor is that my intention. I think there are better resources you can use to unpack that. But since this is a book on gracious disagreement and since, statistically speaking, you also likely know and love someone who is same-sex attracted, then I think this is a relevant comparison. And having worked in the American church for over twenty years, I've seen that this continues to be a paramount conversation. If my relationship with my brother has taught me anything, it's that navigating personal sexuality is a complex thing. It's powerfully complicated. Sex, after all, is one of the most powerful forces on the planet. Last I checked, human beings needed the following things to continue as a species: air, food, water, sleep, and sex. It makes sense that there would be some disagreement surrounding it.

Now, hear me say that I'm not going to try to change your mind on sexuality. After all, this isn't a book about changing your mind on certain things. It's about reconsidering the posture we take when speaking with one another on those things. I've found that if someone is fully convinced that you love them, you are rewarded with permission to speak into places others aren't. I am hoping we all learn to inspect and re-address the posture we unknowingly take toward those whose sexuality appalls or frightens us—or those whose *opinions* about the sexuality of others repel us. After all, many are tempted to say, "Aha! So that's what you think about sexuality. Well, then, now I have an excuse not to love you!"

It's such a white-hot topic these days, and I hope to challenge people on both sides—both those who support and those who oppose same-sex-attracted individuals. Jesus told the story of the good Samaritan to keep us *all* on the hook, so to speak. Wherever your beliefs fall, I'm not saying truth isn't important. What I'm saying is that sometimes, truth in the wrong tone can sound like a warning alarm instead of a dinner bell.

If you hold a more traditional interpretation of Scripture, does it at least hurt your heart to hear that my brother felt he had to distance himself from me out of love? Consider that for a moment. He wasn't trying to protect himself from vicious words or judgment, but he was actively trying to protect *my* Christian musician notoriety. When I heard those words come out of his mouth as we drove to Indianapolis that day, I broke down in tears. My brother's broken heart broke mine. The thought that he didn't think we could be close because my followers would condemn me for it was something I never intended for him. I pray he never feels that way again.

If you hold a more progressive interpretation, would you be open to hearing out someone who doesn't? Is there a place of safety we can build to better hear one another out on this? In other words, what if we all took a hard look at who we consider a "Samaritan"?

JESUS LOVED A BAD REPUTATION

I think the single greatest cause of lack of empathy is that we're too scared to be associated with those we disagree with. This goes both ways. Regarding same-sex attraction, there are folks with a fundamental view who would never dare be lumped together with someone with a progressive view. The same could be said the other way around. As for me, I've concluded that I never want my fear of association to dictate who I will befriend, nor do I want anyone's perception of me to dictate how I will perceive them. I think this is partly the reason the priest and the Levite in the parable walked around the man on the road. They couldn't risk contamination by affiliation. They dared not be associated with him.

But this was Jesus's whole point. He was the most sacred, but He was never concerned with contamination. You'll see this over and over in the Bible. Lepers, prostitutes, bleeding women, demoniacs, centurions, Pharisees—He wasn't afraid of being associated with anyone. He didn't run from them; He moved toward them. If you watch Him closely in the Gospels, you'll see that He didn't seem to believe in such things as Samaritans, though He fully recognized that humanity did. (Of course, I'm using this term as a label. I'm not saying He didn't recognize Samaria.)

Jesus upset everyone on both sides all the time with His unwillingness to disassociate. He'd be hanging with tax collectors and frustrating religious leaders one minute, and then the next minute He'd have dinner with the religious leaders while upsetting the down-and-outs. It's as if Jesus loved hurting His own reputation.

Honestly, I think that's it. If Jesus loves to be close to sinners, then that means Jesus loves a bad reputation. To the Pharisees He asks, "Who is your Samaritan?" To the down-and-outs He asks, "Who is your Pharisee?" It goes both ways. I can't say that enough in this chapter. I want you to see that whatever the issue, the offense comes from both sides. The road to gracious disagreement starts at a different side for all of us, but hopefully, all our paths will one day meet in Jesus.

Now, some of my church friends might call to mind a problematic verse in Thessalonians. They'll remind me that we must "abstain from all appearance of evil," as it says in 1 Thessalonians 5:22 (KJV). I can't tell you how many times I've audibly groaned when someone quotes this verse to me. This can't mean what we initially think, can it? What about Jesus, then? Didn't He keep up all kinds of evil appearances?

The Greek word for "appearance" is *eidos*. Many commentators say it is much better translated into the phrase *form of evil*. That's why the same verse in different versions reads, "Abstain from every form of evil." This is a profoundly helpful delineation between appearance and action. Think on it. If Paul were saying that *appearing* to be evil is a sin, then Jesus would have been guilty as charged. In Luke 7:34 Jesus said, "You say, 'Look at him! A glutton and a drunkard, a friend of tax collectors and sinners!'" If Jesus was worried about keeping up appearances, I don't think He would have come down here and rubbed shoulders with any of us in the first place.

I pray we learn the importance of this. May we never let opinions of others dictate the proximity we keep. Those appearances may just keep us from being the love of Christ to those who need it most.

I WELCOME YOUR COMPLAINTS

You might now be thinking, *So, Mike, are you saying that I have to be best friends with people whose beliefs are radically different from mine? I thought bad company corrupts good character.* Don't misunderstand me. It absolutely can. And I'm not saying your beliefs on things like sexuality don't matter. They do. I'm not saying there are no black and whites when it comes to sexuality. But as Jesus taught us in the parable, sometimes our fear of association can keep us from seeing the neighbors right in front of us. If we're not careful, the lines we draw based on our own convictions can quickly erect fences that end up keeping certain people out. I mentioned my friend Justin McRoberts earlier. I texted him to get his permission to quote him, and when he heard what this book was about, he quickly wrote me, "Taking the tribe God has given you a few steps toward Jesus is brutal and costly and very nuanced. It's way harder than being a radical."

I love that last bit especially. To graciously associate and walk with people is harder than being a radical. In fact, it's truly radical. Nuance is more radical than being radical. If the Pharisees complained that Jesus hung out with sinners, then I sure hope they complain about me. If they complained that Jesus's associations gave Him the look of a drunk and glutton, then may I no longer be afraid of a bad reputation.

I should also say, I'm no longer afraid to be associated with the self-righteous either. Sexual orientation is but one example of how we label others and ourselves. Homosexuals or heterosexuals, chief justices or criminals, prostitutes or preachers, fundamentalists or postmodernists—*identity* is the core issue under it all. No one is a Samaritan, not even me. There is no one above my purity and no one beneath my love. It's level ground here at the foot of the cross. I get to love those who disagree with me. I get to be associated with those who will get me in trouble. I get to love those who boycott me and those whose ideas are radically different from mine. I love those who tell me I need to stand for truth, and I love those who tell me my truth is too strict. I really do get to love everybody.

Of course, the question remains, How do we do that? What does love look like? Isn't love telling someone hard truths even if they don't want to hear it? Does loving someone mean agreeing with everything they believe? Can you even love someone who feels hated every time they're disagreed with? How do I love the souls with differing beliefs, especially when minds are made up on two opposing sides? Where do I draw the lines when the gray begins to bump up against the black and white? How do I build bridges to Jesus and to others? And in what ways could I be unknowingly burning those bridges down? And are there times that my building a bridge creates a pathway for the Enemy to get past necessary defenses?

That's a whole lot of questions that I'm still wrestling to answer, and I hope you are too. I hope we never stop asking the Holy Spirit when to speak and when to listen. Samaritan or Levite, bandit or victim, we all deserve to be heard.

TO HEAR OR BE HEARD

Maybe this sounds bizarre to you, but after the friendships I've built and the conversations I've had, I'm quite convinced that when it comes to the deep places of a person's heart, the privilege of speaking to those things is something that must be built with time and trust. It must be asked for, not thrown down from above. If you recall, Jesus didn't even reprimand the woman at the well. He simply invited her to ask Him for living water. He acknowledged her tumultuous love life, but only after He'd offered her living water. It's also worth noting the Samaritan didn't ask the guy lying on the road what he believed. He just tended his wounds.

I firmly believe it isn't my calling to steward the morality of humankind. I'm simply called to make disciples. And that is a down-and-dirty, one-person-at-a-time kind of a calling. It's small, oftentimes thankless, and it's not a campaign. It's a kingdom intent more on hearing than on being heard. I'm not called to judge the world in the here and now; I'm called to love the world. I'm not even called to change the world—that's the Holy Spirit's job. I'm to simply introduce people to Jesus and let Him do the rest. If He is life, my job should be to bring others to His arms and let the power of His love shift their thinking. I shouldn't be surprised if He's constantly changing my thinking too. I make the introduction, but Jesus wins the heart.

To hear or be heard? If those around us aren't being heard by us, chances are, they won't be exactly chomping at the bit to listen to us. I bet when we put down our megaphones, we'll find a whole world out there waiting to be heard. And when they know we truly want to hear, they just might be interested in what we have to say too.

Jesus was always telling the disciples that they were blessed because their ears worked. I need to remember that. I need to remember my ears hearing is more important than my mouth talking. If I'm not really listening, how will I know what to say anyway? It's worth pointing out that if you read every interaction of Jesus in the Gospels, you probably won't come away with clear-cut evangelism formula. Instead, you'll find a Savior who is custom tailoring His message to the heart of the person He's talking with. This is so incredibly helpful. If the Son of God is listening to all kinds of humans, from all kinds of backgrounds, with all kinds of beliefs, then maybe you can too.

I don't know about you, but I want to live in a world with no Samaritans. Everyone gets a seat at my table, because I get a seat at God's. I want eyes that see and ears that hear. I no longer come to the world with clenched fists; I come with open hands. I do not come with a swinging gavel; I come with a life laid down. I am not the captain of my own ship. I have surrendered all the controls. I don't have to rule the world with my judgments; instead, I get to serve with kindness. Now I get to be a friend to sinners and saints alike. I come to the world the way Jesus came to me. In short, whether Pharisee or Samaritan, I get to embrace everyone.

Wounds from a Friend

"A true friend stabs you in the front."

—often attributed to Oscar Wilde

I love this statement by Peter Bromberg: "When we avoid difficult conversations, we trade short-term discomfort for long-
term dysfunction."[1] A difficult conversation might not feel good in
the moment. It can feel like being pummeled in Ping-Pong or, as
I'll share, being weirdly celebrated on your birthday. But avoidance never cures what ails us. If I go to my doctor, I don't want
him to lie to me. I want him to tell me the truth so I can start addressing the problem. In the same way, we must be allowed to
speak into one another's lives. The more we rest in the arms of a
kind Savior, the less defensive we will become and the more gently
we will correct. Remember the verse in 2 Timothy 2:25 that talks
about "correcting his opponents with gentleness"? We have to stop
worrying about disagreement in terms of winning or losing. Who
cares? Are you fostering real conversation by inviting critique, or

are you squashing your opportunity to grow by denying your friends the chance to point out your flaws? Conflict avoidance undermines intimacy.

I was having a small birthday gathering with some of my closest friends when my friend Ryan exclaimed, "Mike, you make me feel uncomfortable, and that's why I trust you." With that, he kicked off one of the strangest birthday toasts I've ever received in my entire life.

"No, seriously," he went on in a bemused fashion, "if I don't want to hear the truth, I'm definitely not calling Mike."

"Hear, hear! Amen!" A dozen affirmations sounded from around the circle as drinks were raised by my friends. I could feel my ears getting hotter by the second.

"Mike always tells me exactly what he thinks," my friend Zach chimed in to what was quickly turning from toast to roast.

"Mike is a true friend but not the guy who's going to inflate your ego," someone echoed from behind me.

A few more hearty qualifiers were thrown about, and I was left wondering whether I'm a good friend or just an uptight critic.

I circled back with Ryan after the toasting subsided. "Hey, so I'm having some feelings here. Can I ask you something? Do you think I overstep? Do you think I'm a terrible encourager? I don't want to be the guy running people into the ground."

"Of course not," Ryan reassured me. "You're just the guy who we all need in our lives but sometimes don't want."

"Oh . . ." I stared down at the floor. "Thanks?"

"No, no." He remained upbeat. "Thank *you*."

I still wasn't feeling at rest, so I asked one more clarifying question. "Is it okay that I do that sometimes?"

Ryan didn't miss a beat. "Of course it is."

"But why?" I finally squeaked out.

"Because I know you love me, man."

Ryan turned back to the rest of the crew as I let that last sentence wash over me.

That wasn't the most pleasant toast I've experienced, but upon reflection, it might be the one I'm most proud of. As the Bible says, "Wounds from a friend can be trusted" (Proverbs 27:6, NIV). My friends could handle my past intrusions because deep down they knew I loved them.

Wounds from a friend can be trusted. When we really believe someone has our best interest in mind, we can welcome critique in the places we wouldn't have otherwise. We trust that the wounds, uncomfortable as they might be, aren't meant to hurt but to heal. Wounds heal when the hurt is welcomed, but they have a way of festering when we refuse to embrace them. When we're not sure where someone is coming from, it's easy to hold on to the sting of criticism until it rots into bitterness. But when we really believe someone loves us, we can eventually learn to not only endure but even invite criticism. We trust the sting of a surgeon's knife because we believe it is meant to heal us.

EXPANDING CIRCLES

Let me ask, Do you love being told you're wrong? The Bible says that a wise person loves rebuke but a foolish person hates it (Proverbs 9:8, NIV). Think about that verse for a good long minute. The wise love being told they're wrong. Why? Because that's how they learn. You always know when you're sitting across the table from a wise man. He may offer sound defenses for what he thinks, but he never gets defensive. Never. That's a huge difference.

How, though? How do we come to love rebuke? If you're like

I used to be, that sounds impossible. Now that I've had some years working at this very thing, here's my best answer: Start close and work outward. I think if we can just start by hearing from those closest to us, we can learn to invite criticism from gradually expanding circles.

Here's where the shift begins. In the context of relationship, we begin to hear criticism as conversation and not confrontation. Or, I should say, it's possible to hear it that way. If we really believe that the person we're talking to loves us, we can start this process of loving the wounds when they come. This is the circle that can eventually expand into elegant disagreement. Start close and balloon. Start inward and move out.

Begin with the people closest in your life. If we can't learn to disagree with them, we'll never learn elsewhere. Hopefully, in the safety of relationship with a trusted friend, the sting of disagreement is removed. Or it should be, at least. On one hand, those closest to us can hurt us the most. But if a friend is truly safe and truly loves us, although their critique still hurts, there's a purpose for the pain. Maybe we can move from avoiding confrontation to actually pursuing it. And I don't mean we go around picking fights; I mean we look forward to hearing what we can work on.

I believe we can eventually look forward to receiving criticism from total strangers too. But we'll expedite the process by letting our friends in. And I mean real friends, not just acquaintances. Who are they? As I like to say, "You know who your friends are by who will happily give you a ride to the airport when you could just as easily take an Uber." Your friends are the people in your life who you know will joyfully inconvenience themselves for you—no strings attached. Friends are the people we ask, "How does this outfit look?" when we really want the honest truth. Start with those friends. Start with your "ride or die" and maybe you'll find yourself dying less when a stranger unexpectedly shoots you straight.

I'M NOT LOSING; I'M LEARNING

My friend Blake has helped me shift my thinking in this matter. Through him, I've learned to invite criticism in the same way I was dishing it out to my friends unrequested. How does Blake do this? He helps me learn by destroying me at Ping-Pong. I mean, he absolutely decimates me. Not to brag here, but I'm no slouch either. I worked at a church for a long time, so let's just say I can wield a paddle with the best of them. I've spent endless afternoons and coffee breaks working on my Forrest Gump form and challenging every staff member I could. I would even call myself, comparatively speaking, good. But when I play against Blake, I feel like someone replaced my hands with oven mitts. It's like I'm playing left-handed, and the guy doesn't miss. It's maddening. To make matters worse, he casually makes small talk throughout the match, as if crushing me takes zero effort whatsoever. Sure, I may win the occasional game, but by occasional I mean one in ten. That's a 90 percent loss rate, at least! Naturally, I don't take it well. The last time we played, after my seventh or eighth loss in a row, I moaned, "Blake, why do I even play you? There's no point. I'm going to lose, and I hate it!"

Blake's face was covered in sweat, but he wasn't overexerting himself. It was just stifling in the garage. We were playing in southern Florida in the middle of the summer, so sweat just happens. He nonchalantly wiped his fogged glasses in between serves.

"Well, Mike . . . may I be so bold?" Blake began to preach to me as we played.

"Your mindset is all wrong. Give me the ball. Thanks. See . . . wait, what's the score? Oh right. Fifteen serving ten. Here we go. See, your problem is your mindset. My point. Sixteen to ten. When I'm playing someone better than me . . . and I'm definitely better than you—"

"What's your point, Blake?" I interrupted.

"My point is . . . Oh, nice shot. There you go."

"Don't pander to me, Blake."

"Sorry, sorry. But that was a really nice return. You should feel good about it. The point is, when I'm playing someone better than me, I get excited. I don't get mad that I'm losing. I get excited that I have the chance to learn. I'm not losing; I'm learning."

Hmm. I'm not losing; I'm learning.

He beat me that game 21–12. But something switched inside me. Blake was absolutely right. I needed to change my mindset. I needed to change the way I approached the table. I needed to stop coming to the game to win and instead start coming to the game to learn. What's more, I needed to approach my friendships the same way. I needed to think of friendship the way Blake thinks about Ping-Pong.

Makes sense, right? Ping-Pong is a really great image for the way we can talk to one another. We go back and forth. Each person gets a turn. The other party makes a good point.

We argue back, saying, "But did you think about this?"

They counter, "No, but what about this?"

Debate ought to be like verbal Ping-Pong. Everyone gets a turn, and there's a natural give-and-take. If you play against a wall, it's pretty boring. If you play against no one, it's lonely. But if you put your ego aside, you might learn a new trick. If you trust the person on the other end, you don't even mind when you just got served.

DO YOU SPEAK HOLY SPIRIT?

It doesn't take a genius to realize we are far more likely to receive something harsh from someone we trust. When we know someone loves us, it changes everything. But that leads to the question, If no one is ready to receive criticism from me, could it be that I'm the one who needs to change my approach?

In his book *Gentle and Lowly,* Dane Ortlund asks us to consider the heart of Christ toward us sinners. "He is the most understanding person in the universe. The posture most natural to him is not a pointed finger but open arms. . . . No one in human history has ever been more approachable than Jesus Christ."[2] He goes on to point out that Jesus spoke plenty of stern words throughout His time on earth. But if you look closely, you'll see His hard words are for the ones who wouldn't admit they needed Him. This is the same for us. Everyone sounds harsh when we aren't willing to hear.

This might be a bit traumatic if you have incurred some of your deepest wounds from someone you trusted in the name of Jesus. That is completely understandable. The more we trust someone, the more willing we are to hear them, and the deeper they can hurt us. It's a risky paradigm. We all want community, but community requires vulnerability, and vulnerability requires risk. I don't want to minimize the risk of relationship for those of us who are recovering from wounds inflicted by someone we trusted but who, as it turned out, didn't deserve that trust.

However, whatever has happened, healing for our wounds can start when we stop blaming Jesus for what someone did in His name. I do believe the more we rest in the heart of Christ, the more our posture will shift toward the people who have hurt us and the people who don't agree with us. If we really believe that Jesus isn't wagging a finger at us but is opening His arms to us, I think that will change the way we hear His voice when He prods us to change. It might even change the way we speak to others when we offer critique.

Think of the difference between the devil and the Holy Spirit for a moment. Satan is the accuser. That's who he is. It's what he does. He hurls accusations, while the Spirit gently inquires. The Enemy slings arrows, while God prods with sincerity. Have you considered God's first words to Adam and Eve after they ate of the forbidden fruit? He didn't say, "What is wrong with you two? How dare you disobey Me? Why would you do something so stupid?" He doesn't interrogate; He initiates. What He did say was, "Where are you? Who told you that?" The voice of God sounds very different from the voices of condemnation. While the voice of shame screams, God inquires. When you engage in the gray matters, do you ever stop to ask yourself, *What would the Holy Spirit sound like right now? What would He ask? What are the words He would use and the tone He would take?*

If you're having trouble gaining trust to speak into someone else's life, consider this. Just a few days ago, I was out on tour with my friend Joe, lamenting that I wanted to pummel someone online for something they were saying. He gently responded, "Do you speak Holy Spirit? That response just doesn't sound like something He would say." That was all I needed to hear. I'm still thinking about that question as I finish this book. It might be the most important question I could ask you too. It's certainly the most important question I could ask myself: *Do you speak Holy Spirit?*

I would rather be known for who I am than loved for who I'm not. And I would rather be told five words of truth than a thousand words of flattery. It's taken me a long time to get here, but as I've gotten older, I've realized that wounds from a friend really can be trusted. I'm learning to receive correction from Jesus first, then my wife, then my children, then my friends, and then everyone else in my life. Gracious disagreement has a way of spreading like seismic waves from the epicenter of an earthquake. The earthquake is the deep soul knowledge that you are loved despite all the ways you've gotten it wrong. It has a way of shaking the foundations and eventually affecting every relationship we have going outward. With that deep belief, I'm able to say I'd rather learn from my mistakes than bask in the glow of my successes. I hope somewhere in this mess of musings of a book, I have helped convince you accordingly.

I'll close with one last story of a sweet lady who came to a concert of mine. This happened just a few weeks ago, and I'm still buzzing over a simple and profound truth that I think is a perfect thought to leave you with.

I was packing up merchandise in the lobby of a church after a concert, the last stragglers slowly exiting, when this lady asked softly, "What do I do if I'm afraid to make Jesus my lord?" I looked up and saw her eyes filling with tears. It was a bit out of the blue, since my friends had just been talking about songs and concerts and T-shirts. I could see the fear nagging behind her question and her past flickering like a movie in her eyes.

"Oh," I said, taking a second to find the words that felt like something the Holy Spirit would say. "Well, I suppose you should first realize you already have lords. We all have lords, right? Whoever you're giving control to, whatever is filling up your mind and your heart—those people, those things, are already the lords of your life. I don't think Jesus wants to be your lord to hurt you or harm you. In fact, because He knows every other lord will only end up hurting you in the end, He must be asking us to make Him lord because He knows He's the only lord who will truly be kind."

"Wow," she sort of half whispered dreamily, "I'd never thought about it like that. I already have lords."

"Yeah," I encouraged her, "we all do. And He really is the only lord who is kind."

I don't know if that strikes you, but I hope as you close this book, you might close your eyes and ask yourself as honestly as you can, *Who is my lord?* Is it being right? Is it feeling safe? Is it always winning and never showing any signs of weakness? I mean, you picked up this book because you wanted to learn how to disagree better. What was behind that motivation? Whom were you hoping to better understand? I've heard it said that we need to seek to understand before we seek to be understood, but I think we can only stop obsessing over being understood when we feel truly seen and loved. I believe that happens most profoundly when we allow ourselves to be seen through the ever-loving gaze of God.

I think some of us, deep down, are afraid to make Jesus our lord. Maybe we're afraid that will make us weak. Maybe we're afraid of losing arguments. If Jesus is your lord, it's harder to lord over anyone. Or maybe it's because we're afraid He'll disagree with us. But, like my friends told me and like I'm learning to see from my friends, "Wounds from a friend can be trusted." Whoever you let in will end up hurting you. That's how our souls work. The greater the capacity for healing, the greater capacity for hurting too. You can't let anyone in without opening yourself up to injury. As I've said before, that's the cost of relationship. But I'm telling you, friend, Jesus may indeed disagree with you in all kinds of ways, but that's what friends do. They want the best for us, and they're happy to ask us to change if they know that change will bring us life. And, I might add, I know for sure that there is no one else who will disagree with you for all the right reasons. If He's asking you to change, you better believe He knows what He's talking about.

If Jesus is the only lord who is kind, then His kindness, I believe, will trickle down into every area of our lives. His kindness changes the way we talk—it changes the way we do everything. When His kindness runs our lives, we can begin to be kind with everyone, including ourselves. When we can admit we're wrong but aren't defeated by it, we are set free from shame and smug monsters. We are freed to hold the tension. We can stretch. We can kiss the fool looking back at us in the mirror. We can utter the four magic words "I could be wrong." We can speak when we need to and keep silent when we need to. We can pray more honestly and listen more attentively. When our own bitterness becomes the enemy, people are no longer the enemy. We fight differently. We get the forks out of our own blenders at all costs. We become more patient online and in person. We make friends with our feelings, and we lead with curiosity and kindness. We become spacious. We hold space for doubt. We hold space for everyone. No one is a Samaritan. No one is a Pharisee. We take away the labels, and we begin to hear like never before. This is what it means to find grace in the gray.

If you've made this journey, I believe you're on your way. Everything is beginning to look different. You're making the move from enduring disagreement to actually loving people in the midst of it. Welcome. Isn't the view beautiful from here?

NOTES

CHAPTER 1: LEANING IN

1. First We Feast, "Jeff Goldblum Says He Likes to Be Called Daddy While Eating Spicy Wings," *Hot Ones*, August 30, 2018, YouTube video, 18:38, www.youtube.com/watch?v=TMfVEkfXEV8&list=PLAzrgbu8gEMLTBXKb0Bt KDgrR9Qe8UKwe&index=12.

2. Victor Hugo, *Les Misérables*, trans. Isabel F. Hapgood (New York: Thomas Y. Crowell & Co., 1887), 107.

3. Dallas Willard, *The Great Omission: Reclaiming Jesus's Essential Teachings on Discipleship* (New York: HarperCollins, 2006), 61.

CHAPTER 3: GET THE FORK OUT OF HERE

1. Bible Hub, s.v. "5117. *topos*," https://biblehub.com/greek/5117.htm.

2. C. S. Lewis, *The Great Divorce* (New York: Macmillan, 1946), 75.

3. C. S. Lewis, *The Grand Miracle: And Other Selected Essays on Theology and Ethics from God in the Dock*, ed. Walter Hooper (New York: Ballantine, 1970), 110.

4. Brant Hansen, *Unoffendable: How Just One Change Can Make All of Life Better* (Nashville: W Publishing, 2015).

CHAPTER 4: LIVE LIKE I'VE GOT NO ENEMIES

1. *The Usual Suspects*, directed by Bryan Singer (Beverly Hills, Calif.: MGM, 1995).

2. U2, "Invisible," *Songs of Innocence*, Island Records, 2014.

CHAPTER 5: KISSING THE FOOL

1. G. K. Chesterton, letter to the *Daily News*, April 16, 1905, quoted in Stephen Bullivant, "Continuing the Hunt for a Fabled GK Chesterton Quote," *Catholic Herald*, December 17, 2019, https://catholicherald.co.uk/continuing-the-hunt-for-a-fabled-gk-chesterton-quote.

CHAPTER 6: THE SMUG MONSTER

1. T. S. Eliot, *The Cocktail Party* (Orlando: Harcourt Brace & Company, 1950), 31.

2. *Merriam-Webster*, s.v. "smug (*adj.*)," www.merriam-webster.com/dictionary/smug.

CHAPTER 7: THE FOUR MAGIC WORDS

1. Leonard Cohen, "Anthem," *The Future*, Columbia Records, 1992.

CHAPTER 8: HOLDING THE TENSION

1. Bible Hub, s.v. "5315. *nephesh*," https://biblehub.com/hebrew/5315.htm.

2. Tim Mackie and Jon Collins, "You Are a Soul," *The BibleProject*, November 13, 2017, https://thebibleproject.simplecast.com/episodes/0b7f0750.

3. "Nephesh/Soul," episode 5 in *The Shema Series*, video, The BibleProject, http://bibleproject.com/explore/video/nephesh-soul.

CHAPTER 9: ARGUING WITH CHILDREN

1. "Prefrontal Cortex," ScienceDirect, www.sciencedirect.com/topics/medicine-and-dentistry/prefrontal-cortex.

2. Rosamond Hutt, "Women Have More Active Brains Than Men, According to Science," *Business Insider*, April 6, 2018, www.businessinsider.com/women-have-more-active-brains-than-men-according-to-science-2018-4.

3. Jennifer H. Suor et al., "Tracing Differential Pathways of Risk: Associations Among Family Adversity, Cortisol, and Cognitive Functioning in Childhood," *Child Development* 86, no. 4 (July/August 2015): 1142–58, www.ncbi.nlm.nih.gov/pmc/articles/PMC4683120.

4. Joseph Troncale, "Your Lizard Brain," *Psychology Today*, April 22, 2014,

www.psychologytoday.com/us/blog/where-addiction-meets-your-brain
/201404/your-lizard-brain.

5. The Lone Bellow, "You Can Be All Kinds of Emotional," *The Lone Bellow,*
Descendant Records, 2013.

CHAPTER 11: SPEAKING OF SOCIAL MEDIA

1. Timothy Keller, "Social Media, Identity, and the Church," *Life in the Gospel,*
Summer 2021, https://quarterly.gospelinlife.com/social-media-identity
-and-the-church.

2. "Andrew Carnegie: Quotes," Goodreads, www.goodreads.com/quotes
/9423755-men-are-developed-the-same-way-gold-is-mined-when.

CHAPTER 12: FEELINGS ARE OUR FRIENDS

1. Different researchers have come up with different emotion words, but the
idea is generally the same. The words we used in our group were from Chip
Dodd's book *The Voice of the Heart: A Call to Full Living,* 2nd ed. (Nashville: Sage
Hill Resources, 2014).

CHAPTER 13: GRACE IN FAITH AND DECONSTRUCTION

1. Robert Richardson, *Memoirs of Alexander Campbell* (Cincinnati, Ohio: R. W.
Carroll, 1872), 237, www.google.com/books/edition/Memoirs_of_Alexander
_Campbell/YTRGAAAAYAAJ.

2. "The Apostles' Creed," *The (Online) Book of Common Prayer,* www.bcponline
.org/General/Apostles_Creed.html.

3. A. W. Tozer, *The Knowledge of the Holy* (New York: HarperCollins, 1961), 1.

4. Richard Newton, *The King in His Beauty* (New York: American Tract Society,
1878), 5.

5. Donavyn Coffey, "Why Does Christianity Have So Many Denominations?," LiveScience, February 27, 2021, www.livescience.com/christianity
-denominations.html.

6. StudyLight.org, s.v. "*qadosh,*" www.studylight.org/lexicons/eng/hebrew
/6918.html.

7. Kip Wheeler, "What Is *Logos?,*" https://web.cn.edu/kwheeler/documents
/Logos.pdf.

CHAPTER 14: WHO IS YOUR SAMARITAN?

1. "From Jerusalem to Jericho," American Bible Society Resources, https://
bibleresources.americanbible.org/resource/from-jerusalem-to-jericho.

2. Quoted in E. T. Bell, *Mathematics: Queen and Servant of Science* (New York: McGraw-Hill, 1951), 42.

CHAPTER 15: WOUNDS FROM A FRIEND

1. Peter Bromberg, "Purposeful Influence" (keynote presentation, Connecticut Library Association Leadership Institute, Hartford, Conn., August 9, 2013), www.slideshare.net/pbromberg/purposeful-influence-keynote-at-connecticut-leadership-institute-august-9-2013.
2. Dane C. Ortlund, *Gentle and Lowly: The Heart of Christ for Sinners and Sufferers* (Wheaton, Ill.: Crossway, 2020), 19–20.

Mike Donehey has seen his fair share of the unexpected. Following a near-fatal car crash as a teen, Mike learned to play the guitar while in bed recovering from his injuries. Playing the guitar quickly gave birth to songwriting, and that songwriting quickly led to the formation of a band—Tenth Avenue North—which became one of the most loved and successful bands in Christian music. Beginning with their acclaimed national debut, *Over and Underneath*, Tenth Avenue North's audience multiplied with each new album and hit song, like radio favorites "Love Is Here," "By Your Side," "You Are More," "Losing," "Worn," "I Have This Hope," and the multiweek number one smash "Control (Somehow You Want Me)."

At the beginning of 2020, despite widespread fame and a devout following, Tenth Avenue North's members began to sense they each had their own unique roads to follow, and they disbanded.

Mike has seized this opportunity, reveling

in the excitement to expand as a storyteller, communicator, and thought instigator wherever his voice is heard. Mike's first book, *Finding God's Life for My Will*, was widely acclaimed and became an immediate bestseller upon its release. Mike's new podcast, *Chasing the Beauty* on AccessMore, looks for the joy of God in unexpected places. But perhaps most exciting, Mike has written and produced new music for his debut solo album, *Flourish*. Being one of the music industry's most exciting and engaging live performers and speakers, Mike will continue to make live appearances a big part of his story going forward.

The unexpected has a way of disrupting our lives in ways we might not have ever chosen. But for Mike Donehey, learning to embrace the unexpected has been the very thing that has brought forth encouraging and soul-healing art—time and time again. Mike trusts that he will be led in ways that allow him to continue serving and inspiring.

Mike and his wife, Kelly, live in Nashville, Tennessee, with their four daughters.

SUCCEED BY SURRENDERING

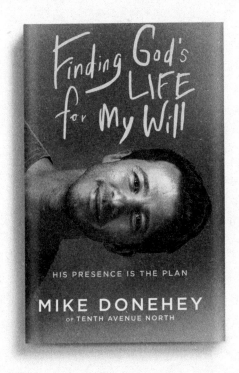

Waiting for certainty from God before making decisions may seem super spiritual, but it can lead to a life of fear, stress, and regret. Stop looking for God's will for your life and start finding God's life for your will.

Learn more about Mike's books at WaterBrookMultnomah.com.